EMB-314 SUPER TUCANO, Brazil's turboprop success story continues

João Paulo Zeitoun Moralez

EMB-314 SUPER TUCANO

Brazil's turboprop success story continues

João Paulo Zeitoun Moralez

HARPIA
PUBLISHING+

Consulting and inspiration by Kerstin Berger

Front cover artwork by Murilo Camargo Martins shows an Ecuadorian EMB-314 Super Tucano from Escuadrón de Combate 2313 (Combat Squadron 2313).

Rear cover artworks by Murilo Camargo Martins; from top to bottom: EMB-314 Super Tucanos of the FAB Esquadrilha da Fumaça, Lebanese Air Force 7th Squadron and Mauritania Super Tucano Squadron.

Artworks by Murilo Camargo Martins

Editorial by Thomas Newdick

Layout by Norbert Novak, www.media-n.at, Vienna

Printed at finidr, Czech Republic

Harpia Publishing, L.L.C. is a member of

ISBN 978-0-9973092-4-9

Contents

Introduction

The instrument panel is equipped with three, colour multifunction liquid-crystal displays with only three analogue instruments provided as back-up in case of malfunction. Communications are encrypted and the aircraft is capable of using conventional or guided weapons and even air-to-air missiles.

Missions can be carried out 24 hours a day with the aid of night vision goggles (NVGs) and a precise navigation and targeting system. For the pilot, datalink, head-up display (HUD), anti-G suit, on-board oxygen generator system, 'hands on throttle and stick' (HOTAS) controls and chaff/flare launchers are also available. As standard, the aircraft is fitted with two 12.7mm (0.5in) machine guns with 250 rounds each and the armour plating for the crew and engine can withstand hits from projectiles up to 12.7mm (0.5in) calibre.

While the above avionics and capabilities might suggest a fourth-generation jet fighter, they in fact describe the Embraer EMB-314 Super Tucano, a single-engine turboprop.

The initial requirements that led to the Super Tucano's development in the early 1990s called for an aircraft specifically tailored for ground-attack, interception, air defence and surveillance in the Amazon environment, i.e. in locations with limited infrastructure and high temperature and humidity, and for training combat pilots of the Força Aérea Brasileira (FAB, Brazilian Air Force). It would be an evolution of the EMB-312 Tucano (see *EMB-312 Tucano: Brazil's turboprop success story*). However, by the end of the project, the similarity between the two aircraft was essentially limited to the name.

The Super Tucano is the result of experience gained in combat operations by nine of the 16 countries that employ the Tucano, chiefly Brazil. Ultimately, the new Brazilian aircraft ended up fulfilling long-standing requirements in many countries.

For several decades, unconventional forces have been the primary enemy for many nations: drug smugglers, guerrillas and terrorists driving off-road vehicles in the desert or in the jungle. Operating a jet fighter is expensive, complex and requires considerable ground support and logistics. They are costly to buy and even costlier to operate.

Even so, many countries have traditionally maintained a heterogeneous force of combat jets to perform various missions – air defence, attack and interception – each calling for different performance and armament parameters. However, by the beginning of the new century, most countries were operating with a limited or very strict defence budget, with a consequent reduction in the acquisition of complex fleets.

A mixed fleet also causes logistic problems, with maintenance and purchase of materiel from different suppliers, and potential for interruption in spare parts supply, for example.

Jets require complex ground support, long, paved runways, and are often based far from the combat area, consuming more fuel and flying time. On the flight line, often no more than half of such aircraft are ready for immediate operation. Because they are expensive to maintain, pilots end up flying fewer hours, reducing their proficiency. Meanwhile, due to high acquisition costs, an aircraft typically remains in service for 30 or more years, gradually becoming obsolete.

For some time now, single- or twin-engine piston or turboprop aircraft have been designed specifically for the counterinsurgency (COIN) mission. These aircraft were

EMB-312 Tucano

6

typically basic and robust. Traditionally, they utilised simple analogue avionics and were unable to carry out attack missions with precision ordnance.

With the emergence of multirole aircraft in the mid-1970s came the potential benefit of unifying all combat tasks in a single platform, with a universal training process, doctrine, maintenance and operations. At the same time, however, these new fighters were much more complex, and very expensive to maintain.

The Super Tucano combined the efficiency and ruggedness of traditional COIN aircraft with fourth-generation avionics. The cost of a flight hour starts at USD 1,000, or a little less depending on variant and operator. The figure is considerably less than that of a single- or twin-engine fourth-generation jet.

For countries facing guerrilla warfare or terrorism threats, it makes little difference whether modern technology is installed on a turboprop or jet. But in terms of acquisition cost, and above all cost of operation, it can be a question of victory or defeat. The cheaper an aircraft is to fly, the more pilots will be able to fly it and the more aircraft will be available to carry out combat missions; alternatively, a few aircraft will be able to fly a larger number of sorties.

When tackling an insurgency, a Super Tucano – taking off from air bases or deployed to airstrips close to the enemy, with little ground support, infrastructure or paved runways – makes more sense than formations of F-16s, F/A-18s or, soon, F-35s. For this type of warfare, rocket launchers and gun pods are generally adequate. In some more specific cases, laser-guided bombs might be useful for attacking targets in dense forest or in caves.

Turboprops do not need to refuel in flight, they can stay longer over the target and at a much lower cost. In case of an accident, the materiel loss is much lower.

Some air forces are able to fly more than 80 per cent of their missions on Embraer turboprops, leaving the remainder for modern fourth-generation jet fighters, but without the need to acquire a large number of such aircraft. Jets can be used as a 'silver bullet' force, a strategic and deterrent reserve.

Among the 13 Super Tucano operators, Afghanistan, Burkina Faso, the Dominican Republic, Lebanon and Mauritania do not use fighter jets of any kind. In Colombia and Ecuador, despite the availability of air superiority fighters, the Super Tucano is now the main combat aircraft, widely used for training and internal security. In Brazil, it is the most numerous combat aircraft operated by the FAB.

The United States is considering the Super Tucano to complement or to replace the Fairchild A-10C Thunderbolt II under the so-called OA-X programme. The Pentagon has also bought 33 Super Tucanos to equip the air forces of Afghanistan and Lebanon.

In peacetime, the Super Tucano's versatility can provide all necessary training for future jet pilots. For the newly trained military pilot, it can teach the use of datalink, NVGs, HOTAS, HUD, electro-optical/infrared systems, radar warning receivers, chaff/flare, within-visual-range and beyond-visual-range missile launch doctrine, and the architecture of a modern 'glass' cockpit fighter. The Super Tucano can provide tuition in all the systems found in a jet fighter, but at a considerably lower cost than a lead-in fighter trainer.

Acknowledgments

The Super Tucano is a strategic aircraft used by many Air Forces and to ascertain the operation and particularity in each country where it is used was challenge and required a wide network of contacts.

I would like to express my deepest gratitude to Colonel Rinaldo Nery, an experienced attack pilot on the EMB-312 Tucano, who has been one of the key participants in Brazilian aviation history and for the development of the EMB-314 Super Tucano in particular. His collaboration allowed access to other people and sources which helped me to uncover important historical facts for this work.

To my friend Murilo Camargo Martins, the best illustrator I have had the honour to know, for the fantastic technical achievement in the artworks enhancing this book. Each of his completed illustrations fills the eyes with beauty. His contagious enthusiasm and his attention to emblems and other details of the Super Tucano were an inspiration and enabled me to find out more information for the text itself.

To Coronel Aparecido Camazano Alamino, a friend who always opened his files and shared his knowledge with me so that the work could be as complete as possible.

To my wife Nathaly and my daughter Amália, my inspirations for this project and whose company I had to sacrifice for this work.

Not all of them could be mentioned here, but I expressly thank the 1°/3° GAV, 2°/3° GAV, 2°/5° GAV, 3°/3° GAV, Colonel Budhi Achmadi (Indonesia), Esquadrão de Demonstração Aérea, Aparecido Camazano Alamino (Brazil), Angolan Air Force, André Luiz Bandeira (Brazil), Rubens Barbosa (Brazil), Sergeant Johnson Barros (Brazil), Sergeant Bruno Batista (Brazil), Brazilian Air Force, Chilean Air Force, Mark Condeno (Philippines), Tom Cooper (Austria), Colombian Air Force, Detikom, André Oliveira Duailibi (Brazil), Neil Dunridge (United Kingdom), Ecuadorian Air Force, Centro Histórico Embraer, Embraer, Corporal Feitosa (Brazil), Renzo Galuppo Fernandes (Brazil), Francisco Ferro (Brazil), United States Air Force, Sergeant Leonardo Garcia Gaedke (Brazil), Lieutenant Márcio Inforzatto (Brazil), Admiral Cristóvão M. da Silva Júnior (Angola), Major Ubirajara Pereira Costa Jr. (Brazil), Petty Officer Waldemar Prieto Júnior (Brazil), Lieutenant Enilton Kirchhof (Brazil), Maurício Lanza (Brazil), Ary Guilherme Leber (Brazil), Corporal Silva Lopes (Brazil), Carlos Lorch (Brazil), Sergeant Paulo Marques (Brazil), Force Aérienne Islamique de Mauritanie, Força Aérea magazine (Brazil), Tecnologia & Defesa magazine, Sergeant Manfrim (Brazil), Sergio Menezes (Brazil), Mauro César Mezzacappa (Brazil), Vatche Mitilian (Lebanon), Colonel Rinaldo Nery (Brazil), Diego Oliveira (Brazil), Paulo César Pinheiro (Brazil), Luciano Porto (Brazil), Andrés Ramírez (Colombia), Sergeant Paulo Rezende (Brazil), Sergeant Diego Sodré Ribeiro (Brazil), Santiago Rivas (Argentina), Colonel Wagner Rocha (Brazil), Guilherme Kozien Roczon - speedalive.com.br (Brazil), Dax Román (Dominican Republic), Lieutenant Camila Oliveira Sampaio (Brazil), Parque de Material Aeronáutico de Lagoa Santa (Brazil), Sérgio Santana (Brazil), Corporal V. Santos (Brazil), Colonel Gilberto Schittini (Brazil), Sergeant Tiago Martins da Silva (Brazil), Sergeant Simo (Brazil), Colonel Taufik (Indonesia), Katsuhiko Tokunaga (Japan), João Vaz (Angola), Luiz Fernando Nolf Ventura (Brazil), Mario Vinagre (Brazil), Instituto de Pesquisas e Ensaios em Voo (Brazil), Pit Weinert (Germany) and Andreas Zeitler (Germany).

Abbreviations

AACMI	autonomous air combat manoeuvring instrumentation
AAF	Afghan Air Force
ADF	automatic direction finder
AEW&C	airborne early warning and control
AFA	Academia da Força Aérea (Brazilian Air Force Academy)
AHRS	attitude and heading reference system
ANA	Afghan National Army
APKWS	advanced precision kill weapons system
AQIM	al Qaeda in the Islamic Maghreb
BFAF	Burkina Faso Air Force (Force Aérienne de Burkina Faso)
BVR	beyond visual range
CAS	close air support
CCIL	continuously computed impact line
CCIP	Constantly Computed Impact Point
CCRP	continuously computed release point
cm	centimetre
CMFD	colour multi-function display
COIN	counterinsurgency
CRT	cathode ray tube
CTA	Centro Técnico Aeroespacial (Aerospace Technical Centre)
DCTA	Departamento de Ciência e Tecnologia Aeroespacial (Brazilian Department of Aerospace Science and Technology)
DME	distance measuring equipment
DTC	data transfer cartridge
DTOS	Dive Toss
EDA	Esquadrão de Demonstração Aérea (Air Demonstration Squadron)
EFIS	electronic flight instrument system
EICAS	engine-indicating and crew-alerting system
EO/IR	electrical-optical/infrared
FAB	Força Aérea Brasileira (Brazilian Air Force)
FAC	Fuerza Aérea Colombiana (Colombian Air Force)
FACh	Fuerza Aérea de Chile (Chilean Air Force)
FAD	Fuerza Aérea de República Dominicana (Dominican Air Force)
FADEC	Full Authority Digital Engine Control
FAE	Fuerza Aérea Ecuatoriana (Ecuadorian Air Force)
FAIM	Force Aérienne Islamique de Mauritanie (Mauritanian Air Force)
FANA	Força Aérea Nacional de Angola (Angolan Air Force)
FARC	Forças Armadas Revolucionárias Colombianas (Revolutionary Armed Forces of Colombia)
FARM	Force Aérienne de la Republique du Mali (Mali Air Force)
ft	feet
GAV	Grupo de Aviação (Aviation Group, Brazil)
GCI	ground control intercept
GPS	global positioning system
GPWS	ground proximity warning system

HF	high frequency
HMD	helmet-mounted display
HOTAS	hands on throttle and stick
HUD	head-up display
IFR	instrument flight rules
ILS	instrument landing system
in	inches
IPEV	Instituto de Pesquisas e Ensaios em Voo (In-Flight Research and Testing Institute)
IQT	initial qualification training
km	kilometre
km/h	kilometre per hour
LAF	Lebanese Air Force (Al Quwwat al-Jawwiya al-Lubnaniyya)
LAS	Light Air Support
lb	pounds
LCD	liquid crystal display
m	metres
MDC	mission and display computer
MDGT	mission data ground terminal
MDS	mission debriefing station
MFD	multifunction display
MPS	mission planning station
mph	mile per hour
MQT	mission qualification training
NATO	North Atlantic Treaty Organization
NDB	non-directional beacon
NFTC	NATO Flying Training in Canada
nm	nautical miles
NVGs	night vision goggles
OBOGS	on-board oxygen generator system
PAF	Philippine Air Force (Hukbong Himpapawid ng Pilipinas)
PoC	Proof of Concept
RFI	request for information
RFP	request for proposal
RPM	rotation per minute
RWR	radar warning receiver
TCAS	traffic collision avoidance system
TNI-AU	Tentara Nasional Indonesia-Angkatan Udara (Indonesian Air Force)
UHF	ultra high frequency
UN	United Nations
USAF	United States Air Force
US Gal.	United States gallon
USN	United States Navy
VFR	visual flight rules
VHF	very high frequency
VOR	very high frequency omnidirectional range
WVR	within visual range

ROADMAP TO THE SUPER TUCANO

To understand the history of the Embraer EMB-314 Super Tucano it is necessary to piece together a multitude of fragments which would eventually culminate in the design of what is arguably the most versatile, flexible and advanced modern combat turboprop.

Almost five years after the EMB-312 was introduced into service with the Força Aérea Brasileira (FAB, Brazilian Air Force) and with some other air forces around the world, including Argentina, Egypt, Honduras, Iran, Iraq, Paraguay, Peru, the United Kingdom and Venezuela, suggestions for its improvement began to emerge resulting from its operators' experiences, the ever-changing global geopolitical context, the formation of new threats, advances in technology and new operational needs in training and combat.

As the performance of the EMB-312 was explored and its range of missions expanded, more suggestions were aired and more and possibilities became clear.

Unlike the EMB-312, which was devised with the specific mission of serving at the advanced training segment at the FAB after the retirement of the Cessna T-37C, the paths that lead to the EMB-314 were various, but they ultimately converged.

Initial thoughts at Embraer

As we described in our book *EMB-312 Tucano – Brazil's turboprop success story*, the evolution of the Tucano started within Embraer itself. The company was eager not to lose its share of the market to competitors such as the Pilatus PC-9, an aircraft that received a steady stream of improvements, and became superior to the basic Tucano.

EMB-312 PT-ZTW c/n 312.161 received a 1,100shp Garrett TPE 331-12B with a four-blade Hartzell propeller and a dive brake, for trials of an improved version of the EMB-312 Tucano. (Mauro César Mezzacappa)

A late 1980s illustration showing the EMB-312 flying a COIN mission with heavy armament. This version was a single-seater and was planned to carry armour plating. (Archive João Paulo Moralez)

Based on the Royal Air Force Short Tucano project, EMB-312 c/n 312.161 registered as PT-ZTW, had its nose modified to receive a 1,100shp Garrett TPE 331-12B with a four-blade Hartzell HC-B4TN-5S/T9327K propeller, plus a dive brake.

Designated EMB-312 G-1 and described in study TD-312/734, of September 1985, fatigue life would be increased to 15,000 hours and the G-load factor would rise to +7/-3.6. In addition there would be new avionics, a new canopy and increased load capacity at the four wing stations. Because it was similar to the Short Tucano itself, Embraer believed that sales potential would be weak and that the variant would compete with the Short Brothers version.

Embraer then considered an even further improved version of the Tucano for combat/armed use, with digital cockpit, HUD, a reinforced structure for increased armament capacity, new avionics, diving brake, a new canopy and higher G-load capacity and fatigue life. With the FAB's intention to equip attack squadrons with the EMB-312, the G-1A variant, as it was known, would be the ideal and most suitable solution.

In parallel, however, a third variant was envisaged. Initially dubbed Helicopter Killer, the model would be a single-seater with Kevlar removable armour on the cockpit sides, a floor able to withstand up to 7.62mm (0.3in) hits, digital cockpit, HUD, self-sealing tanks, laser rangefinder, rocket pods, fire-and-forget missiles and a 20mm GIAT cannon. The aircraft would have a fuel tank installed in the space traditionally reserved for the instructor on the EMB-312, at the rear nacelle, extending its autonomy and flight range. The engine would be the 1,100shp Pratt & Whitney PT6A-67/13.

Together with the FAB, Embraer tested the features that this aircraft would have to employ against a helicopter, a doctrine that was later was developed and incorporated into the 2ª Esquadrilha de Ligação e Observação (2nd Liaison and Observation Flight, 2nd ELO) in the mid-1990s. The trial involved the modified PT-ZTW with Garrett engine and dive brake, an EMB-312 and a Helibras HB-350 Esquilo (a Brazilian-built AS350 Écureuil), the latter two from the then Centro Técnico Aeroespacial (CTA, Aerospace Technical Centre). The aim was to evaluate the Tucano's flight qualities and performance in this type of mission; the application of tactics and techniques of air-to-air combat against helicopters in a dissimilar warfare scenario and to establish what would be the kind of weapons necessary in this type of confrontation.

It was from the G1A/Helicopter Killer combination that the EMB-312H evolved. It was a single-seater which could withstand G-loads of +8/-4, had 12,000 flight hours of fatigue life, increased weapon loadout capability, cockpit and engine armour resistant to 7.62mm (0.3in) hits at distances of 100m (300ft), larger wheels and more robust brakes, updated zero-zero ejection seats, anti-G for pilot, 2.5psi (0.17bar) pressurised cockpit, air conditioning, 1,125shp Pratt & Whitney PT6A-67/17 engine with Full Authority Digital Engine Control (FADEC) driving a four-blade propeller.

As for the avionics, there was an HUD with Weapon Aiming Computer, an Air Data Computer, video recording system and attitude and heading reference system (AHRS) and Constantly Computed Impact Point (CCIP). This was the general framework of report PT-312H/962 of September 1988.

JPATS – The American Dream

The early 1970s saw the US Air Force (USAF) procuring a new primary training aircraft for its cadets.

It had, since 1958, been using the Cessna T-37B twin-engine jet as the second aircraft with which cadets would have contact throughout their training.

As a primary trainer, in fact, the T-37B was versatile, robust and efficient. However, it was already showing signs of obsolescence and, in addition, the USAF was predicting that its fleet of Cessna trainers would soon suffer a significant reduction in the availability and quantity of aircraft.

Structural attrition was enormous. Each aircraft flew a high average of 500 hours a year, each hour costing USD 400.00. According to USAF forecasts, its T-37B fleet would be shut down in the late 1980s, primarily for structural reasons, when most of its examples would already have reached their 15,000 hours of fatigue life.

Thus, in the late 1970s, the USAF launched Next Generation Trainer (NTG), a programme to replace its T-37Bs. In general terms, the weight of the new aircraft would range from 2,267kg to 2,721kg (5,000lb to 6,000lb), would employ a side-by-side cockpit, and have two engines of 1,000lb thrust each (later changed to 1,500lb) and a cruising speed of 556km/h (300kts).

Cessna was one of five competitors offering a replacement for the its T-37B. Another option proposed by Cessna would be the modernisation of the existing fleet to the T-37D standard.

In mid-1982 Fairchild won a contract worth USD 104 million to build two flight prototypes, two ground structural tests airframes and up to 54 production units.

Construction of this initial batch of Fairchild T-46s – a twin engine, twin tail (similar to the A-10) and high wing – would begin in 1984 with the 54 airframes delivered by 1987, when the first T-37B would leave active service from USAF.

However, developing the T-46 presented several costing problems and the weight of the aircraft increased, affecting its performance. After many setbacks, the programme was cancelled on 13 March 1987. In turn, the USAF invested in a 537 T-37B structural life extension programme valued at USD 114 million, which extended fatigue life by more than 8,000 hours through kits provided by Saberliner Corporation and installed by the air force itself from 1994.

From individual to joint operations

In April 1988 the USAF published the Air Force Trainer Master Plan, which stated that cadets would begin training on a primary jet platform such as the T-37B, before moving on to specialise on fighter-bomber aviation or transport. To do so, three new aircraft models would be needed. These would be to replace the T-37B for the primary flights, the T-38 on fighter-bomber missions, and to supply a new trainer for in-flight refuelling and other training.

For its T-37B replacement the USAF created the Primary Aircraft Training System (PATS), which required an 'off the shelf' aircraft with the fewest modifications possible to meet deadlines and keep to a low budget.

Heavily modified PT-ZTW served as a Proof of Concept for the JPATS programme. It incorporated a 1,600shp Pratt & Whitney PT6A-67R with five-blade Hartzell propeller, fuselage length increased by 1.37m (54in), a new spinner, and other modifications including new landing gear doors, new ailerons, a ram-air intake on the rear fuselage, a new fin fillet fairing, as well as a larger, higher tail, trim rudder and OBOGS.
(Archive Colonel Aparecido Camazano Alamino)

At the same time, the US Navy (USN) T-34C fleet had already given ten years of training, and the service could foresee the requirement for a new primary training aircraft to replace it from 2000 onwards. At that point, the oldest aircraft would be close to completing 25 years of operations. This presented an opportunity to conduct a unique programme serving both armed forces and, at the same time, fulfil a new demand from the US Congress that requested, whenever possible, that the same training platform serve the two forces.

PATS was renamed as the Joint Primary Aircraft Training System (JPATS) in January 1989 when requirements were jointly written by the air force and the navy.

Those requirements specified that the JPATS aircraft should have sufficient fuel capacity for four types of instruction flights: contact, navigation, training and instruments, plus a 463km (250nm) landing alternative. The cockpit should be pressurised to 3.5psi, with advanced avionics and as many digital instruments as possible and should also allow for instrument flight with UHF/VHF communications, as well as GPS, an Instrument Landing System (ILS), Distance Measuring Equipment (DME) and VHF omnidirectional radio range (VOR).

The ergonomics of the aircraft should allow 80 per cent of those people eligible to be air force or navy pilots, both male and female, to fly in the JPATS aircraft, ranging in height from 1.53m (5ft) to 1.97m (6ft 6in). A liquid oxygen system and a ten-litre capacity reservoir or, preferably, an on-board Oxygen Generator System were also requested.

The canopy must withstand 1.8kg (4lb) birds at speeds of 550km/h (300kts) at 42°C (108°F), but it was desirable for it to withstand the same mass at 500km/h (270kts). It should also withstand wind speeds of 46km/h (25kts) on take-off.

The minimum fatigue life was to be 15,800 flight hours over a period of 20 years, with an average of 60 hours per month, and a monthly maximum of 65 hours, while supporting fatigue loads of +6/-3G. It was desirable that the structure could withstand 19,000 hours of life over 24 years. The ejection seats, mandatorily, should have zero/sixty capability, and eject at ground level with a speed of 60kts (110km/h). However, a zero/zero seat was preferred.

The aircraft should have a maximum of 3.2 man/hours maintenance for each flight hour.

Attentive to this requirement, Embraer decided to modify the PT-ZTW with an existing 1,100shp Garrett engine to a new 1,600shp Pratt & Whitney PT6A-67R with five-blade Hartzell propeller while at the same time increasing the fuselage length by 1.37m (54in). The aircraft received a large air intake on the left side of the nose to cool the engine oil, a new spinner and modifications ventrally, such as new landing gear doors, new ailerons, a ram air-intake on the back for heat exchanger, a new fin fillet fairing as well as a larger and higher tail and trim rudder.

The programme was officially launched at Embraer in January 1991 and on 9 September of that year the aircraft made its inaugural flight under the command of test pilot Colonel Gilberto Schittini and flight test engineer Mauro César Mezzacappa. The flight lasted 1h50 and the aircraft reached a speed of 463km/h (250kts) and an altitude of 3,500m (11,482ft).

Called the Proof of Concept (PoC), or EMB-312H, the aircraft was projected to demonstrate that in practice the new airframe could meet the demands and requirements of JPATS.

Embraer, however, was experiencing difficulties. There were no funds, and the state-owned company that once had 10,000 employees was reduced to only 3,000 at that time. Through a huge effort by the FAB, the company was kept alive with payrolls unaffected, until better winds blew again.

As Schittini recalled:

'The PoC and then the JPATS prototypes were made at Embraer, but with one detail. They were not built normally like any other prototype. They were made in the maintenance of the test flight department. The engineer responsible for coordinating the project was Sérgio Horta; system changes were made by Emilio Kazunoli Matsuo; manufacturing and assembly workshop was the responsibility of Klaus Kurz and the test engineer was Mezzacappa. The manufacturing style was like [Lockheed's] Skunk Works. We gave our blood to make the planes. The PoC was welded to the floor of the Embraer Flight Testing hangar. We cut it in half, inserted another meter (3.28ft) in the fuselage behind the cockpit, 37cm (14.56in) in the front and a 1,600shp engine. We changed fin and rudder, which got higher. The PoC and the two subsequent prototypes of the programme cost only five million dollars.'

PP-ZTV was the first JPATS prototype constructed by Embraer. It incorporated a new PT6A-68/1 engine, a new electrically operated vertical-opening canopy, digital cockpit, GPS, TCAS and anti-G. (Mauro César Mezzacappa)

PT-ZTW also incorporated OBOGS, EMB-120 Brasilia's air-cycle air-conditioning system and pressurised fuel supply.

The changes were made at low cost and in six months.

To choose the painting scheme of the aircraft Embraer promoted an internal competition among its employees and the winner was engineer Renzo Galuppo Fernandes. The aircraft would be painted blue with a yellow ray on the side of the fuselage. The story goes that, for lack of money, the blue paint was the same one used to paint the tools at Embraer. The aircraft was known as *Ana Raio*, because at the time a Brazilian television channel was airing the soap opera *'Ana Raio e Zé Trovão'* (Ann Lightning and Joe Thunder).

In 1989, knowing that the US would soon officially open the JPATS, Embraer began talks with McDonnell Douglas for a partnership if its product was to be the winner. But in July 1990 the negotiations were discontinued and in January the following year conversations concerning JPATS were initiated with General Dynamics. A team was in Fort Worth to see the F-16 assembly line and during the conversations, doubts were raised if a student could move from an elementary trainer – the Cessna T-41 – to an aircraft with 1,600shp of power.

The doubt, however, was solved when two students who were graduating at the Aeroclube of São José dos Campos, flew *Ana Raio* without any problems.

Following the decision of McDonnell Douglas, General Dynamics also gave up on the partnership and, ultimately, Embraer partnered with Northrop for JPATS. Embraer would develop the tooling, the fabrication of the entire metal structure, the subassemblies, transportation and testing of special equipment. Northrop would undertake the assembly line, test flights and deliveries.

Two Northrop flight test engineers, Daniel T. Grossman and Hector A. Negroni, as well as test pilot Jackie C. Jackson, flew on 30 May 1990 with Embraer's demonstration Tucano, EMB-312A PP-ZTK, a conventional variant with a 750shp engine and whose pilot was Colonel Schittini. Flight results indicated that the aircraft had excellent stability on all flight axes, with equally good stall and post-stall characteristics, a good instrument platform and solid manoeuvrability. On the other hand, the natural stall warning was barely noticeable and the aircraft was underpowered for JPATS.

The second prototype for the JPATS programme was PP-ZTF. After the competition, it was used to develop the Brazilian ALX that later led to the Super Tucano. Here it appears with three external fuel tanks and two Mk 82 bombs.
(Carlos Lorch, Revista Força Aérea)

The team also flew on the EMB-312H (PoC), describing its superior performance and excellent pilot-in-the-loop with good stall and spin characteristics, directional trim with power variation and seat-pin warning. On the negative side it had non-linear power response, resulting in negative power 'bites' and some handling problems.

The aircraft was superior to the PC-9 and was competitive for JPATS. According to the Northrop report, to win the competition, the EMB-312H should have a FADEC (Full Authority Digital Engine Control) to create a smooth and linear response in power variations, as in a jet, in addition to having a damping trimmer to provide the characteristics and feeling of flying a jet. To meet JPATS requirements, the cockpit should be pressurised and should employ a canopy with a vertical opening (clamshell) and an emergency explosive jettison system as well as a new avionics suite.

Embraer then made a series of modifications on the EMB-312H, naming it the Super Tucano. In May 1992 a protocol of intent was signed with Northrop, and on 27 July EMB-312H, together with PT-ZTT, – a conventional and unmodified EMB-312 – flew to the US to complete training, promotional and demonstration flights for both the USAF and the USN. In total there were almost 100 hours of demonstrations in 83 flights.

With the results obtained, two more prototypes were built which incorporated almost all the requirements established in JPATS, including every modification made in the PoC and reinforcements of the fuselage. They also incorporated a new PT6A-68/1 engine, a fully refurbished canopy with an electrically-operated vertical opening and emergency jettison system, a new cockpit with more cathode ray tube (CRT) digital instruments, GPS, TCAS and anti-G. Fatigue life was to range from 15,600 to 18,700 hours bearing loads of +7/-3.5G.

The first prototype with all these JPATS modifications flew on 15 May 1993 as PP-ZTV (later PT-ZTV). In July, Embraer and Northrop officialised their partnership, and from 6 to 9 September, demonstration flights to USAF and USN officers took place. These comprised 14 missions, 16 flights and 82 landings with the aircraft accomplish-

ing 29h05 of flight. In October, Embraer would fly a second example of the JPATS prototype, PP-ZTF (later PT-ZTF).

Embraer, however, did not succeed with JPATS. In June 1995, Pilatus, in partnership with Beechcraft, won the competition to provide 372 T-6A Texan IIs to the USAF and 339 to the USN, at a total value of USD 4 billion. The costs during the fleet's life cycle were expected to reach another USD 7 billion.

Nevertheless, following JPATS, Embraer won a significant competition to equip NATO Flying Training in Canada (NFTC), with 26 aircraft. The programme, which was devised in 1994, was multilateral with the participation of the Canadian government through the Royal Canadian Air Force in partnership with the Defence Systems Division led by Bombardier and a consortium signed by CAE Aviation, ATCO Frontec, British Aerospace Military Aircraft and Embraer. The Super Tucano would be employed for the basic training which would eventually qualify military pilots for their future aviation roles: air combat, helicopter or transport. Following the announcement of the winners, which also included the BAe Hawk for the advanced training flights on the jet pilot course, the Super Tucano and Hawk flew together for an advertisement photograph.

However, as a protest, Bombardier – Embraer's main rival in the segment of regional transport aircraft – refused to buy Embraer's Super Tucano in favour of Beechcraft's T-6 Texan II.

A second chance

While Embraer was involved in JPATS and in a struggle for its survival in the deep crisis of the 1990s, the motivation of two young lieutenants of the FAB would lead the company to design an aircraft which would be even better than the two prototypes developed for the American competition. The so-called ALX programme emerged and it would ultimately become the Super Tucano which conquered 13 air forces around the world and, at the time of writing, is about to be chosen by the USAF as a possible substitute for the Fairchild A-10 Thunderbolt II for CAS in low-intensity conflicts.

According to Air Force Academy instructor Colonel Rinaldo Nery:

'It was in one of Wagner Rocha's trips to São José dos Campos (SP) that he, a lieutenant and instructor like me at the Air Force Academy (AFA), saw the JPATS' prototype at Embraer and started talking with the flight test pilot, Gilberto Schittini, about a possible armed version of that aircraft. We had a lot of experience in the armed employment of the EMB-312 Tucano in 2ª ELO. It was there that everything began, both in the employment in operational missions of the Tucano and in the reactivation of attack aviation at the FAB. Schittini told Wagner to put something on paper and show him. Then he went back to the Academy and told me what had happened and asked if I did not want to write this document with him.'

The genesis of the Super Tucano project actually started in a very informal way from the bottom up, rather than appearing as a demand from the Air Force General Staff to meet an operational need or deficiency.

The lieutenants' ideas coincided with the thoughts at Embraer, which since the late 1980s already envisioned an armed version of the Tucano, dedicated to specific attack missions. JPATS and the attack variants were parallel projects, but the priority for

PP-ZTV was used to demonstrate a range of weapons, including this multirole configuration. In this instance, the aircraft is carrying a SUU-20 training pod, two Mectron MAA-1 Piranha missiles and two pods for 19 unguided rockets each. (Carlos Lorch, Revista Força Aérea)

Embraer was the US programme which would provide a new lease of life for the company if it should win.

Colonel Nery again:

'So we started to draw what the plane could have. Exhaust heat suppressors, self-sealing tanks, cockpit and engine armour, gyro-stabilised sight, GPS, low-pressure tyres to operate on unprepared runways, chaff/flare launchers, storm scope, communication systems more suitable to a jungle environment, four internal weapons inside the wings, being two 12.7mm (0.5in) and two 7.62mm (0.3in) machine guns. There would be wingtip tanks to extend the radius of action and time over the enemy and six external points for weapons under the wings.

All these features would be essential for operation in the Amazonian environment. We made a drawing of the EMB-312 with the modifications, typed everything on the computer, printed the five pages and took it to Embraer. We were still lieutenants. And we went to talk to Anastacio Katsanos, who was in charge of Embraer's Market Intelligence.

Sitting at the table were, Katsanos and Nilton Medina and we started talking about aviation, about the Fairchild A-10, the Douglas Skyraider, the Rockwell OV-10 Bronco, the Embraer AMX and other models. Our thinking was based on the Vietnam War, in that operating environment. There was a gap in the Amazonian environment by the FAB. Katsanos was very impressed and began to involve Engineering, which in turn began to discuss technological issues and solutions of which we had no knowledge. The plane was growing.'

Unintentionally and without this specific knowledge, the five-page document written by the lieutenants was in fact the description of an Operational Need (OpN). The notion of what features the aircraft needed to have formed this technical document.

Brigadier Fernando Mendes Nogueira, then commander of the AFA, became aware of the conversations between the lieutenants and Embraer and he put them in contact with Brigadier Nelson de Souza Taveira, then head of the Coordinating Commission of the Combat Aircraft Programme (COPAC) managing development, acquisition and modernisation of aeronautical material and systems for the Aeronautics Command.

Colonel Nery continued:

'Brigadier Nogueira pushed us into a room together with Brigadier Taveira and said that we had an idea and something to say:

- Brigadier, Embraer is making the JPATS ...

- I know!

- We had an idea, perhaps the FAB may have an opportunity to make an armed version of the plane.

- Explain!

- We were there and even wrote a little paper...

- Let me see the paper! Here's the story: next week you're going to Brasília, to COPAC'

'We got the mission of writing the Preliminary Operational Requirements (POR) of the aircraft and DCA-400-6 helped us to prepare the document, how to write it, what steps we should take. The DCA-400-6 is the Bible of all acquisition processes within the Air Force. In the early 1990s it was small and began to be based on documentation from USAF itself. It addresses the life cycle of aeronautical systems and materials. This document involves several Air Force commands. We went to Brasília specifically to receive instructions from COPAC about the POR.

We then commented with Katsanos that we had this mission and he promptly came to assist us. We received some information from the engine, the Pratt & Whitney PT6A-67R and Wagner began to write down what the specific fuel consumption would be and, with that and considering a central point in Brazil, to imagine the aircraft's radius of action for each type of weapons configuration and flight profile. The Amazonian region was in vogue, for at that time ECO '92, the United Nations Conference on Environment and Development, had taken place at Rio de Janeiro.

The POR was sent to COPAC, to the Aeronautical General Staff, Research and Development Department and the General Command of Air Operations. We delivered it with our own hands. When we arrived at the 3rd Sub-office of the Aeronautical General Staff, at the Planning and Weapons System Section, some colonels were in a meeting and waiting for us. Among them was the head of the 3rd Sub-office that awaited us, Colonel Mendes Ribeiro. We did a presentation of the project and at the end the colonel told us: the Air Force is not dead! Let's get this document the lieutenants did, and we'll make the requirements before we get hit by the facts. Let's work fast!

What did he mean? Embraer was in a crisis with USD 400 million in debt. It would push the JPATS into the FAB making few modifications to the project, but not the way we had asked.'

The FAB's interest in a well-specified project with requirements made to meet 100 per cent of its needs had some justification. At the time the Amazon was devoid of any air combat units, operating only light and medium tactical transport aircraft. Border deployments were complex issues since aircraft had to leave from the south, southeast

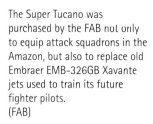

The Super Tucano was purchased by the FAB not only to equip attack squadrons in the Amazon, but also to replace old Embraer EMB-326GB Xavante jets used to train its future fighter pilots.
(FAB)

and midwest to meet any emergency. This would often take hours to achieve, thus losing the advantage of a rapid deployment mission.

In 1992, when the lieutenants' ideas began to coalesce, there were no reconnaissance and attack squadrons in the Amazon Basin, such as those which began to emerge in 1993 equipped with the EMB-312 Tucano, which, in spite of its versatility, was still not the most ideal aircraft for that scenario. The arrival of these Tucano-equipped squadrons in the Amazon Basin were already part of the Amazon Surveillance System (SIVAM), which set up a series of actions to monitor, protect and defend the Amazon area through the integration of several public agencies, ministries, radar installations and modern aircraft, both surveillance and attack. The Super Tucano would be the teeth and claws of SIVAM.

The Amazon Basin is a vast and inhospitable environment. Austria, Belgium, Bulgaria, Denmark, England, France, Germany, Greece, Italy, the Netherlands, Norway, Poland, Portugal, Scotland, Spain, Sweden and Switzerland would fit perfectly into its total area of 5.2 million km^2 (2.07 sq. miles) – 60 per cent of the Brazilian territory. It contains 15 per cent of all surface water on the planet and more than 22 billion trees, some of which weigh as much as 700kg (1,543lb) and reach 80m (262ft) in height. Some of its moth species measure up to 30cm (11.8in) across the wingtips and there are beetles which are almost as big.

Flying over the Amazon is not unlike being over a desert or an ocean. During hours of flight one sees only trees and rivers, with few clearings, towns, villages and only rarely cities. Today, landing strips are relatively easily found, but in the early 1990s there were fewer, many of them still unpaved.

Considering that borders were the main focus of attention, there would be little choice of aircraft for the FAB to make. Among the models in its fleet, only the Embraer AMX and the AT-26 Xavante were viable options to be used in the region because they were subsonic, meaning more runways were available to them. But a jet, in addition to being more expensive and difficult to operate, demanding a very complex infrastructure, would need runways which were paved and at least 2,700m (8,858ft) long in wet conditions or 1,500m (4,921ft) when dry. There were only 13 usable runways and even so, considering the limited range of jets, not all borders would be covered.

The FAB's need for a new aircraft to meet those specific demands was clear: jets were not suitable for operations in a region with limited infrastructure and available runways, and there was no available turboprop type able to fulfil the mission.

As Colonel Nery recalled:

Until the arrival of the modernised F–5EM/FM fleet and the Super Tucano itself, the AMX fleet was the most advanced aircraft available in the Brazilian Air Force inventory. (Corporal V. Santos, FAB)

'In Brasilia we went to Colonel Moura to help us with this mission to improve the POR document we had done. Because the FAB was considering retiring the AT-26, he suggested that we include the fighter pilot training mission in the POR. It was not what we had thought in the beginning.'

By including this mission for the aircraft, the FAB would have a single aircraft type serving two segments, which would make the development and purchase processes easier.

Modern fourth generation fighter jets require 80 per cent of an operational mission to be dedicated to systems management and the remainder to the flight itself. Thus, in economic terms of development, acquisition and operation, an advanced technology turboprop that could introduce the future pilot to the operation and management of the electronic systems of a fourth generation fighter had many advantages over a jet trainer in terms of costs and required infrastructure, despite the jet's superior performance. Understanding the operation of the digital architecture, the next step would be the AT-26 Xavante, in which the pilot would make the transition to supersonic flight, needing just a few hours of flight to achieve this. The rest of the training would be more specific to the squadron mission, developing advanced doctrines and skills.

The recommendation of the POR document was the Super Tucano, as the EMB-312H had already been called since 1992, to complement the military pilot's training in the initial stages of flight at the FAB, equipping the 2°/5° GAV 'Esquadrão Joker' (2nd /5th Aviation Group 'Joker Squadron') where pilots would learn to manoeuvre the aircraft like a war machine by practicing aerial shooting, ground shooting, launching bombs and rockets, as well as air-to-air combat and other basic principles. The 2°/5° GAV AT-26s would pass to the 1°/4° GAV 'Esquadrão Pacau' which would specialise in forming flight and squadron leaders, while at the same time the pilot would learn to fly jet aircraft. Operational life of the AT-26 Xavante would therefore be increased due to less intense use. But there were two problems.

In the late 20th century the FAB was flying in fully analogue cabins. There were no radar-guided missiles or more sophisticated weapons other than short-range, heat-seeking weapons. EFIS, HUD, HOTAS, integrated avionics were all First World technologies which were distant from a country like Brazil. There were only two areas where this reality was present: in the three AMX squadrons – one in Santa Cruz, Rio de Janeiro, and two in Santa Maria, Rio Grande do Sul. More than 95 per cent of the FAB (including the decision-makers) had no experience with these systems and was averse to new technologies and it would require an intense campaign of persuasion

In an another configuration, EMB-314 PP-ZTF demonstrates its ability to carry out combat air patrol missions with Mectron MAA-1 Piranha air-to-air missiles.
(Carlos Lorch, Revista Força Aérea)

to assure them that a turboprop trainer (and related technology) was a good substitute for fighter aviation training. The future aircraft would come into service in the late 1990s, when it was believed that the FAB would be in the process of evolution and the modernisation of its resources. These would include modern cockpits with advanced avionics and this technology would have to be included in the pilots' instruction. Sooner or later, the FAB would have to change its concepts.

Fighter aviation did not take favourably to using a turboprop to train pilots who would fly the future supersonic fighters of frontline aviation but a question remained to be asked. Is it preferable to fly a jet-propelled T-25 Universal or a turboprop F-16? The T-25 Universal jet was, in this case, the AT-26 Xavante, which, except for a pressurised cockpit, ejection seats, higher performance and weapons-carrying capability, was technologically similar to the T-25 basic training aircraft used at the Air Force Academy. The turboprop F-16 was exactly the aircraft which was thought ideal to equip the FAB – meaning an evolution of the EMB-312H. In a nutshell, the technology of an F-16 in a turboprop.

At that time, the turboprop's fuel consumption was a third of that of the jet, increasing its range and enabling it to reach remote points of the borders, while operating from small airfields with unprepared or asphalt runways. In addition to the simple infrastructure needed to operate anywhere in the Amazonian environment, the aircraft would incorporate many of the JPATS' planned modifications.

It is fair to say that the general concept of the Super Tucano resembles that of a Block 60 F-16. However, it is a docile aircraft with good flight qualities and is simple and forgiving – an ideal student aircraft, therefore.

On 18 August 1995, a development contract was signed between Embraer and the FAB. It was for 148 single- and two-seater aircraft which would be destined for five combat squadrons and one fighter pilot instruction squadron.

Initially, the aircraft's canopy was to open vertically, controlled electronically, although this was abandoned by the FAB due to acquisition and operation costs and maintenance complexity. The seats would be in an unconventionally higher position, thus keeping the pilot's eyes high above the engine cowling, and giving the sensation of flying a jet fighter, where the radome can be hardly seen. To increase comfort, the cabin received a 5.0psi (0.34bar) pressurisation and a new air-conditioning system which resolved a weak point of the old EMB-312. It would have anti-G for the pilots, since its use was directed to the training of the fighter pilots, and a canopy resistant to impacts of 1.8kg (4lb) birds at speeds of 500km/h (270kts). The new aircraft would be equipped with FADEC and would incorporate the HOTAS system.

Incidentally, for this use as a training platform for fighter pilots, the aircraft's structure was exponentially enhanced when compared to the Tucano. The wing and structure of the EMB-314 are very strong and can withstand heavy loads from manoeuvres required in the training of FAB fighter pilots, following a standard similar to that used with AT-26.

The entire Xavante flight profile served as the basis for the fatigue life of the EMB-314. The wing then gained a central section to increase resistance, not a single, one-piece structure as on the EMB-312, being directly attached to the fuselage. In the armed configuration, the aircraft would be able to receive G charges of +3.5/-1.8.

Avionics may have been the biggest breakthrough of the Super Tucano when compared to all other aircraft of its category at that time. Except for the use of radar, it incorporates all the technology of a fourth-generation fighter.

The Super Tucano system is visualised modularly, a principle which enables immediate replacement of defective components and allows the aircraft to return to the flight line with minimum delay.

The Mission and Display Computer (MDC) is the centrepiece of the avionics system, receiving and processing information from all flight gear, including communication, navigation, weapons, HOTAS, sighting, alarms, datalink, HUD, Colour Multi-Function Display (CMFD), the fuel system and performance calculations. Communication is made through two MIL-STD-1553B data buses, as well as ARINC-429 and EIA-RS-422 bars. The MDC is coupled to the Engine-Indicating and Crew-Alerting System (EICAS) that warns of changes in the normal parameters of the engine and particularly in the electrical and hydraulic systems.

The pilot also has available an HUD with a 24 degree field of view and colour recording camera, which provides the view ahead with the HUD data. Next to it, a keyboard allows the insertion of data for the mission and control of some of the aircraft's systems.

In addition, two 15x20cm (6x8in) CMFDs centred on a 10x10cm (4x4in) display, called Basic Flying Instruments (BTI) allow the redundancy of instruments such as airspeed indicator, attitude, altitude and bank. There are also vertical speed, artificial horizon and G-force meters.

The choice of digital screens was a factor in reducing operational costs, since it would not be necessary to have any CRT screens or analogue versions of each instrument. The digital screens would have everything necessary integrated by software, easing maintenance and lowering costs, as well as allowing greater flight availability. And the ALX screens would be the same as those used in the modernisation of the F-5E/F and Embraer AMX jet fleets. This would allow for the purchase of greater volumes of the same material and also for standardisation, further lowering maintenance and operating costs.

A further advantage is that the same avionics in these models would allow rapid transition from one aircraft to another.

The aircraft is equipped with a digital audio and voice recorder with Ethernet connection, which can record from three video channels (HUD, CMFD and FLIR), two of them simultaneously. Data is saved on an 8GB main memory card with a capacity of 120 minutes if two sources are used (audio and video) and four hours for a single source.

Along with the Autonomous Air Combat Manoeuvring Instrumentation (AACMI), pilots can carry out mission debriefing on the ground at the Mission Data Ground Terminal (MDGT) by viewing each flight parameter, voice and still, following the aircraft's trajectory, altitude and speed in each second of the flight.

Also with the MDGT it is possible to plan the mission by configuring exactly how the flight will proceed. This includes messages which will be used via datalink, flight areas, established routes, communication frequencies, navigation, cockpit screens, chaff/flare configuration, electronic warfare, Identification Friend or Foe (IFF) and others. The MDGT data is inserted into the 128MB Data Transfer Cartridge (DTC) which is placed in the aircraft by the pilot, on the right-hand side of the cockpit.

Also installed are an autopilot, storm scope, altimeter radar and inertial navigation systems. With GPS it is possible to use a current flight plan and to store another 25, all of which have 30 references. There is also a DME, VOR, Localiser (LOC), Marker Beacon, Transponder, Glideslope, ILS and Automatic Direction Finder (ADF). Communication systems include datalink with 10MB/s transmission capacity.

The tactical radio is the Rohde & Schwarz XT 6313D V/UHF with encrypted data and voice transmission. In VHF, it has a frequency range of 225,000 MHz up to 399,975 MHz. For longer distances an HF-ALE is used.

To provide avionics and system-wide integration, following a rigorous selection process, Elbit Systems was chosen, and the contract signed in April 1997. Programme development was at zero cost to the FAB.

The cabin is compatible for operation with third generation night vision goggles, since in jungle regions light is very low and illegal flights of drug dealers and weapons and merchandise smuggling typically occur at night. An interception light mounted on the right side of the engine cover allows the pilot to see the registration of another aircraft between 70m (230ft) and 100m (328ft) distance.

The cockpit has armour protection for the pilots, able to withstand 12.7mm (0.5in) angled impacts. The structure is conventional and made of aluminium, with rudder, landing gear covers and other access panels in composite materials. Unlike the Tucano, it has an auto-rudder which is engaged when the aircraft reaches 90km/h (50kts), thus sparing the pilot of the effort of keeping the aircraft aligned on the runway using the pedals. The rudder is 100 per cent balanced to counteract the flutter effect. Controls are designed to be manual, with increased sturdiness to avoid the need of maintenance in remote locations. With electronic systems stored in an air-conditioned compartment within the aircraft, tests predict that they can operate in humid and hot environments for long periods.

The engine's air intake is designed to reduce the chances of ingesting debris and additionally, in the air duct, there is an inertial separator reducing the odds almost to zero.

The pilot needs only one minute for the aircraft's external inspection before taking off. Ground crews need only ten minutes for pre-flight checks and work no more than an hour and a half on maintenance on the ground for each completed hour of flight. It takes 20 minutes at most to refuel and reload the aircraft with any weapon system and another 30 minutes for post-flight checks.

To decrease refuelling time the Super Tucano is equipped with a central refuelling point; however, it also has points for conventional gravity refuelling.

Considering the lack of infrastructure, OBOGS does not require oxygen cylinders on the runway. Thus, in a combat scenario, the Super Tucano can make several operational sorties in one day, producing a maximum war effort.

The aircraft can land anywhere an earthmover can reach, to create an unpaved runway. The low-pressure 134psi (9.24bar) tyres help the aircraft to operate in these situations and to improve communication with the ground crews, two points for intercom connection are installed, one under the left wing and another under the root of the right wing, near the connection for the external power source.

In emergencies, assuring the continued operation of the aircraft is of fundamental importance, and to this end, the main battery can run for 30 minutes with the aircraft's essential systems remaining in operation, including HF radio, BTI and an engine start. The reserve battery has a two-hour operating life with basic flight systems in addition to the HF radio and one attempt to start the engine.

Another advantage is that the main battery can give three attempts to start the engine, even with its capacity reduced to 70 per cent. If it still does not work, it is possible to directly connect with another Super Tucano through cables, eliminating the need for off-site maintenance in a remote location or border region.

In the event of a forced landing, the Emergency Locator Transmitter (ELT) is activated to provide the aircraft's location for SAR teams, emitting a 406.025 Mhz signal for 24 hours and then at 121.5/243.0 for approximately 72 hours.

The aircraft is equipped with Martin-Baker MKBR10LCX ejection seats, the front seat adopting a trajectory to the right and the rear seat to the left. The canopy has an explosive cord that weakens the transparent section and allows the ejection of the seat through the Plexiglas.

As for ordnance, initially there were to be four external points but these were soon increased to five with a combat load of 1,550kg (3,417lb).

In one of the several visits that Lieutenants Nery and Wagner made to Embraer, a proposal was made to include machine gun pods under the wings. Several models were shown, but the decision was made in favour of FN Herstal's 12.7mm (0.5in) Heavy Machine Pod.

The pilots rebutted, however, saying that the weapons should be organic to the aircraft, a part of it. This would reduce aerodynamic drag and free external points under the wings for other ordnance. On the other hand, the ALX had limited fuel capacity and losing internal space for the machine guns would further compromise its range.

The prototypes and pre-production airframes for the Super Tucano programme included YA-29 5700 to test the single-seat variant.
(Centro Histórico Embraer)

The idea was accepted by Embraer and with support of the FAB's War Material Centre in Rio de Janeiro, they managed to borrow a 0.5in machine gun. With it two moulds were made in Styrofoam and Embraer installed them in the wings, in place of the leading-edge light. To develop the concept of having ammunition bays in the wings, engineers went to the Aerospace Museum in Rio de Janeiro to study two aircraft: a Republic P-47D Thunderbolt and a Curtiss P-40. The latter, in the opinion of Embraer engineers, exemplified the state-of-the-art of wing machine guns. To solve the problem of internal fuel load which was exacerbated by the machine guns, the internal tanks were enlarged.

This soon became one of the distinctive features of the EMB-314 that reduced aero-dynamic drag and increased ordnance load and range, as the tanks could be part of the configuration to accomplish long-range missions while maintaining considerable combat capability. Each machine gun can carry up to 250 rounds. In case of any problems with the ammunition, it is possible for the pilot to re-engage the process, which takes only 15 seconds.

The avionics of the new aircraft would be equipped with CCIP, Continuously Computed Release Point (CCRP) and Continuously Computed Impact Line (CCIL).

Situated ventrally, ahead of the cockpit, and away from the leading edge, and thus allowing a better field of vision, the pilot would also be able to use a Star SAFIRE I, II, III and BRITE Star III FLIR sensors to capture conventional and infrared images, and there would be provision for a laser designator and rangefinder.

On 28 May 1999, the YA-29 FAB 5700, a single-seater variant of which the FAB intended to acquire 50 units, was formally presented to the authorities and the press at its headquarters in São José dos Campos. This aircraft was the former PT-ZTF (c/n 312.455) which participated in the JPATS competition and was converted to the ALX

prototype. It was the first prototype of the programme to fly, taking off at 12.30 on 2 June under the command of Marcos de Oliveira Lima, when it reached an altitude of 1,828m (6,000ft) and a speed of 314km/h (170kts). Unfortunately, this aircraft crashed on a test flight on 1 August 2000 and was subsequently preserved at the Embraer unit in Gavião Peixoto.

Two generations, side by side. Here it is possible to identify most of the differences between the EMB-312 Tucano and the EMB-314 Super Tucano. In practical terms, they are two completely different aircraft, similar only in name.
(Carlos Lorch, Revista Força Aérea)

The EMB-314 production line at Embraer's Gavião Peixoto facilities.
(Centro Histórico Embraer)

The YAT-29 FAB 5900 was the second prototype of the programme, this one being the two-seater variant which first flew on 20 October 1999. A third example of the YA-29 FAB 5701, was built to replace FAB 5700.

The production contract with the FAB was signed on 7 August 2001, initially for 76 single-seater aircraft but with options for another 23, with production starting in early 2002 at the Gavião Peixoto plant. Later, the FAB exercised its purchasing options with 33 examples of the A-29A (as the single-seater version was called in the air force) and 66 A-29B variants (two-seaters, the version with FLIR capability).

However, operation of the infrared system can be carried out only with a second crew member in the rear seat, making it impossible for the A-29A single-seater to have this capability.

Table of prototypes, pre-production and demonstrator aircraft

C/n	Submodel	Registration	First Flight	Situation	Remarks
312.161	G	PT-ZTW	28 July 1986	Preserved	Embraer demonstrator for EMB-312G, similar to Short Tucano, to be offered to Brazilian Air Force and other markets as a more capable aircraft with superior combat support. It was modified to EMB-312H, for the JPATS competition in US. The first flight in new configuration was made on 9 September 1991. Now preserved at MAB Museum, at São José dos Campo (SP).
312.454	H	PT-ZTV	15 May 1993	Scraped	The first ALX program prototype, which transformed into Super Tucano, retained the c/n of the EMB-312 family. First with civilian registration PP-ZTV and then PT-ZTV. Used for flight campaign, withdrawn from use and disassembled.
312.455	H	PT-ZTF	14 October 1993	Scraped	Second flight prototype of the ALX program, using also the EMB-312 c/n. 5700. Restored, maybe using parts from 312.454, YA-29 5700 and the ground tests airframes. Preserved at Gavião Peixoto (SP).
314.99801	A	YA-29 5700	6 February 1999	w/o	Crashed 1 August 2000 at Taubaté (SP) during a test flight.
314.99802	B	YAT-29 5900	22 October 1999	Preserved	Preserved at MAB Museum, São José dos Campos (SP).
314.99803				Scraped	Static ground test structure
314.99804				Scraped	Fatigue ground test structure. Donated to UNITAU University for studies and classroom in late August 2015.
314.99805	A	A-29 5701	21 September 2001	Preserved	Preserved at Museu Aeroespacial (Rio de Janeiro) on 4 August 2011.

AMAZON WARRIOR

SIVAM – Understanding its origins

As incredible as it may seem, until the 1990s the Brazilian Amazon region still did not 'belong' to Brazil, when seen as a region which was not yet properly monitored, controlled and integrated. Beginning with the airspace, the entire Amazon region as well as part of the midwest and the northeast region had no radar coverage to enable the control and monitoring of illegal flights which, as a result, could operate freely throughout the country. On the ground, the situation on the so-called dry frontier was even worse, being described as a Gruyère cheese with its many holes to enable the smuggling of drugs, goods and small arms.

In terms of natural resources, the lack of surveillance also opened the door for the illegal exploitation of mineral, animal and vegetable resources.

As already explained, the Amazon is not an easy environment to monitor and control and nature itself has helped to conceal illicit activities. There are almost 16,000km (9,941 miles), or the distance from Tunis to Cape Town, of shared borders with ten countries. Despite the efforts of the Brazilian Army, there are no human resources available to stop illegal actions in areas where sunlight frequently cannot reach the ground through the tree cover.

Standing with arms crossed was not an option. After involving several government organisations and elaborating a study detailing the concerns over the Amazon Basin and the northern region, in 1990 the Office for Strategic Affairs of the Presidency presented a document emphasising the importance of integrating these regions into the rest of the country. As in the fight against terrorism, victory in that case could be achieved only by involving a large number of offices, organisations, institutions, internal and public security forces and ministries which, working together, could achieve the objectives.

On 21 September 1990, these recommendations were approved along with the Amazon Protection System (SIPAM), which would coordinate the actions of several government departments. But in practice, it would be the sensors and radar installed across the region which would assure the success of the surveillance service. The technology would include meteorological control, conventional and satellite communication, installation of fixed and mobile radar and control of air space over the entire area. The Amazon Surveillance System (SIVAM) was born, and became the eyes and ears of the SIPAM.

The FAB would also have its own eyes and ears. And also its teeth. Early warning and control (AEW&C) and remote sensing aircraft, respectively E-99 and R-99, would be responsible for monitoring both illegal airspace and ground actions with their ELINT, SIGINT and COMINT systems. Initially the fighting element would be in charge of two attack and patrol squadrons equipped with Embraer EMB-312 Tucanos as part of the SIVAM and also as part of a new FAB strategy for the Amazon Basin which would begin in 1993. Thirteen years later, however, these platforms would give way to the Super Tucano.

Designated as A-29A, 33 single seat variants were purchased, each with an extra fuel tank installed in the rear seat position, and 66 A-29Bs, each with two seats to enable training and use of the Star SAFIRE II FLIR image capture system.

To date, only one A-29A has been lost in an accident against nine A-29Bs, totalling ten aircraft in 13 years of operation (2004–17). Major maintenance inspections, modification, structural overhaul and more complex and specific services are carried out by the Parque de Material Aeronáutico de Lagoa Santa (PAMA-LS, Lagoa Santa Aeronautical Material Park), located in the metropolitan area of Belo Horizonte (MG). The site also provides courses and meetings with other operators of the A-29 at the FAB.

2°/5° GAV 'Esquadrão Joker' – Where fighter pilots are born

Armed with two pods of 19 70mm (2.75in) rockets each and a ventral fuel tank, a two-seater Super Tucano from 2°/5° GAV 'Esquadrão Joker' demonstrate its capability in the ground attack mission.
(Sergeant Manfrim, FAB)

The 'Joker Squadron' is the FAB unit responsible for the training course of fighter pilots in Brazil. Until the arrival of the Super Tucano in September 2004, training of Brazilian combat pilots was made in the Embraer EMB-326GB Xavante subsonic jet, a veteran which had completed more than 30 years in service with the FAB. Because the

Joker Squadron is a unit dedicated to instruction, most of its aircraft have high totals of flight hours and greater operational fatigue due to the instruction activity.

In anticipation of the arrival of the Super Tucano, on 3 February 2003, the FAB created the Alfa Group with ten experienced pilots and 20 graduates who would bring the A-29 into service. In practice, this meant writing the whole doctrine of instructions using the new platform. Anything that could be adapted from the Xavante to the turbo-prop was welcomed, but the technological gap between the two platforms meant that few elements could be lifted from one aircraft to the other.

After the pilots had made their conversion to the new aircraft the intense work on introducing it into service with the FAB began.

In the pre-digital era, the student planned his mission using maps unfolded on a large table, marking the points of interest, routes, altitudes, enemy presence and targets on it. The map was carried by the pilot along with a clipboard containing flight data. It was very much a manual undertaking.

In the A-29 this work began to be done in MPS in digital form. Maps, tables, and clipboards were no longer physical items inside the aircraft, since everything was inserted in the A-29's on-board computer via DTC. The MPS also calculated landing distances according to the external load of the aircraft, the amount of fuel and operating altitude, pressure and take-off temperature, and it supplied the pilot with accurate information during its operation.

The computer navigates, correcting wind action and providing detours due to weather or enemy presence on the route. The pilot would manage only the systems, focusing on the fulfilment and the efficiency of the mission, the use of the armaments, the communications via datalink, etc. The flying itself was no longer the main focus.

2°/5° GAV 'Esquadrão Joker'
Ala 10, Natal
2004–today (A-29B)

The Embraer E-99 AEW&C platforms are indispensable for joint operations and to secure Brazilian airspace in the Amazon region.
(1°/3° GAV 'Esquadrão Escorpião')

Members of the Alfa Group also felt the difference between the Xavante and the A-29 in its precision gunnery. The Xavante demanded a lot from the pilot, who focused on a series of internal and external parameters to ensure the accuracy of his attack. In the A-29, automated on-board systems act to place the bomb, rocket, or machine gun bullets at the target shown on the HUD, thus eliminating the need to check flight parameters and to look down to the flight instruments.

Upon returning from a mission, the MDS and AACMI allow in-depth flight analysis at each stage, including the use of weapons, and accuracy of the attack. While it was previously necessary to wait for the development of films from the Xavante's 16mm gun cameras, now it is possible to extract data from the DTC immediately after the flight and carry out two-hour debriefings. It is also possible to include in the same arena up to four participants and to understand the actions and positions of each one through the AACMI.

A curious fact is that only the three operational A-29 squadrons of the Third Aviation Group use the HF radio at the FAB. In other units the system was withdrawn due to lack of use and because it represents an increase in weight of around 40kg (88lb).

In the 2°/5° GAV machine guns are installed only when the student will actually use them operationally. In this way the equipment is preserved, extending its lifespan and also reducing weight in missions where it will not be used.

The Fighter Course

After leaving the Air Force Academy, aspirants selected to take the FAB's fighter aviation course go to Natal where they complete an internship of ten months during which they fly about 150 hours in the Super Tucano.

Here, a one-month Technical Aircraft Instruction Course marks the beginning of the students' training in which they receive theoretical instruction about the aircraft's main systems, normal and emergency procedures and daytime flight manoeuvres. This stage is completed with five tests.

A two-seat Super Tucano from 2°/5° GAV 'Esquadrão Joker' releases two BAFG-120 (128kg–282lb) bombs on the target during the fighter pilot course at Natal.
(Sergeant Manfrim, FAB)

A pair of A-29s from 2°/5° GAV 'Esquadrão Joker' during a training sortie. Most of these operations are conducted by the FAB using two-seat aircraft. (Katsuhiko Tokunaga/D.A.C.T. Inc.)

Flight is divided in a basic module with daytime adaptation (landing, take-off and basic flight manoeuvres), night-time adaptation (the same as daytime adaptation), flight using advanced instruments (airfield landing under adverse conditions using instruments), basic formation (manoeuvres with two aircraft), operational formation (tactical formation in operational flights), navigation by contact (visual flight following ground references for navigation) and radio navigation (using the on-board system of the A-29).

After this, the aspiring pilot enters the advanced module to use the A-29 as a weapons platform. This module is divided into air-to-ground phase (using all conventional weapons available for the FAB's A-29s), air-to-air (attacking with machine guns a target towed by another A-29), air combat (basic manoeuvres 1x1), interception (vectored by radar controllers), operational attack (as wingmen, in a context of real war), escort (in enemy territory with the engagement of enemy forces) and real usage (employing real weapons in a simulated war context).

The FAB's A-29s do not have chaff/flare dispensers, so the students have little contact with the system, and are restricted only to theoretical instructions of their use. Because it does not have the synthetic training package either, it is not possible for students to receive simulated radar images through CMFD or train in missile launching or RWR, chaff/flare as, for example, in Chile and Ecuador.

At the end of the course the trainee is elevated to the rank of 2nd Lieutenant and is declared an Operational Wingman, being able to fly in the wing position (No. 2) in a formation of two aircraft and No. 4 in a flight with four aircraft.

By this time the 2nd Lieutenants are able to move on to one of the three air defence and attack squadrons deployed in the Amazon Basin and midwest, where in their first year they will specialise as fighter pilots.

Defending the dry frontier

The strong arm at the Brazilian dry frontier are the three FAB attack squadrons (considered fighter units at the FAB) of EMB-312 Tucanos, which converted in 2006 to the new platform developed by Embraer, the Super Tucano.

Known as the 'Third' Squadrons, the Third Aviation Group, consists of 1º/3º GAV 'Esquadrão Escorpião' (1st/3rd Aviation Group 'Scorpion Squadron'), 2º/3º GAV 'Esquadrão Grifo' (2nd/3rd Aviation Group 'Griffin Squadron') and the 3º/3º GAV 'Esquadrão Flecha' (3rd/3rd Aviation Group 'Arrow Squadron'), whose headquarters are at the air bases of Boa Vista, Porto Velho and Campo Grande respectively.

The flight and mission's routines include a variety of tasks including attack, escort, interception, CAS, air defence and forward air control. They are also where novice pilots, Operational Wings formed by the 2º/5º GAV will specialise and be ready to fly on the so-called first line air defence aircraft – currently Northrop F-5EM, AMX A-1 (and A-1M) and, in the future, the Gripen E/F.

Developing doctrines

While the 2º/5º GAV in Natal created the so-called Alpha Group to deploy the Super Tucano for the formation of fighter pilots, the Bravo, Charlie and Delta Groups were created in the 1º/3º GAV, 2º/3º GAV and 3º/3º GAV respectively, each with six pilots. Training began with Bravo and Charlie groups, with Ground School carried out at

Ground personnel load a single-seat A-29A with 70mm (2.75in) rockets carried in a seven-round underwing pod. Note the extra fuel tank in the rear nacelle. This adaptation is no longer offered by Embraer, and Brazil is the sole operator.
(Archive 3º/3º GAV 'Esquadrão Flecha')

Embraer headquarters in São José dos Campos for 45 days at the end of 2004. In October 2005 these 12 pilots went on to receive all hands-on training with the 2°/5° GAV instructors in Natal, as they had already accumulated many hours of experience and flight time on the attack aircraft.

One of the pilots who participated in this stage and who asked to remain unidentified reported that:

'After two weeks filled with flights through the skies of the northeast, the pilots already operating on the aircraft departed at the end of October 2005, with three A-29 for each squadron, heading for their bases in Porto Velho and Boa Vista. During the last months of 2005, after receiving the first aircraft, the work pace of members of Bravo and Charlie groups was very intense, since they had to minister Ground School to the rest of the respective squadrons' pilots, as well as perform a big bundle of missions with the aircraft.

These missions had two goals. First was gaining the experience needed to drill aerial instruction to the other squadron pilots, since all members of Bravo and Charlie groups should become instructors themselves. Second, was to test the aircraft in the various employment modes and types of mission, in order to create the A-29's operational doctrine in the Air Force.

The following year, 2006, began with the aerial adaptation of the other pilots to the new aircraft with a rigid schedule, in order to render the entire squadron operational on the aircraft from the beginning of July. At the same time, Embraer's new A-29 deliveries began to occur more frequently, and pilots were required to go to the factory in Gavião Peixoto to pick them up.

Delta Group started implementation of its Super Tucanos in the 3°/3° GAV only after the unit moved from Santa Cruz (Rio de Janeiro) to Campo Grande, first initiating adaptation to the new scenario, with new doctrines and performance. Only after this stage did the group follow the same steps as the Bravo and Charlie groups, receiving their first A-29Bs in May 2006.

Brazilian Air Force A-29 operations include forward-based airstrips close to the border with minimum infrastructure. Here, a 230kg (507lb) BAFG-230 bomb is unloaded from A-29B 5926. (Sergeant Rezende, FAB)

Due to the great distances involved when flying over the Amazon, and the remain to stay on station, it is common for the A-29 fleet to use underwing fuel tanks and the internal 12.7mm (0.5in) machine gun as its main armament.
(Sergeant Johnson Barros, FAB)

The 1°/3° GAV was assigned with the responsibility of developing the entire night vision goggles' doctrine, 2°/3° GAV with use of the Star SAFIRE II FLIR and 3°/3° GAV with use of the datalink. One of the A-29's pilots recalls:

'At the same time that the most advanced missions were carried out during the day, adaptation flights with NVGs also began. Some instructors had already exchanged with the Colombian Air Force and had the opportunity to operate this type of equipment. This way, a flight doctrine was gradually developed with the NVGs, first only with on-board instructors, beginning with take-off missions, touch and go, instrument procedures and landing, followed by navigation at 304m (1,000ft) of height. Starting from that, all the pilots of the squadron made their adaptation to the equipment, fact that changed the unit's routine, since some flights began to be scheduled to 02.00, depending on the moon's luminosity.

At Campo de Provas Brigadeiro Veloso (CPBV, Brigadeiro Veloso Weapon Range), at Cachimbo, in 2006, we did the first air-to-ground missions using NVGs, and the chosen mode of employment was Strafing.

The mission was planned for four A-29Bs and eight pilots. Around 21.00 we were equipped, adjusting the NVGs very carefully. Take-off happened an hour later, and the rendezvous went smoothly.

We then set off for the vector of the firing range and, after a few minutes of adaptation to brightness, the squadron leader ordered dispersion with 10-second intervals between the A-29.

Initially, we made 'dry runs' over the target, only to improve adaptation to night flight and to train speed, height and dive point parameters and also fire and recovery. The squadron leader then gave the command to stand by, at which point we did what was necessary to use the machine guns, only leaving the 'Master Arm' switch turned off.

When my turn came, I reached the correct position in the line and began the dive into the axis of attack. I placed my 'pipper' on the target and switched the 'Master Arm' on, unlocking the guns and waiting to reach the intended distance. So I pressed the trigger and at that moment a huge flash appeared on the NVGs, outshining the HUD's data and the surrounding landscape'.

By 2007, the squadrons of Boa Vista and Porto Velho had acquired sufficient knowledge with NVGs on the range and with inert exercise weapons. It was time for the next step. For this, launching of BAFG-230 (248kg-546lb) bombs using NVGs was proposed, on the CPBV tactical firing range.

The squadrons moved to Cachimbo to carry out armed employment, including a nightly campaign for all pilots. The basic idea was to arm an A-29B element with a BAFG-230 bomb, navigate the CPBV area, and then return to drop the bomb at the tactical range near the runway.

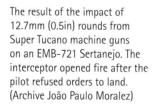

The 12.7mm (0.5in) machine guns are suitable for the majority of air operations. Here, a single-seat A-29A Super Tucano displays its internal armament and the banner with the emergency frequency in case of interceptions.
(Cb V. Santos, FAB)

Destruction Shot

For every hour of every day, the Third Group squadrons have pilots and ground crews ready, waiting to be activated and to accomplish any mission. Two aircraft are kept fuelled and with their machine guns loaded, but because Brazil does not face any external or internal threat, as is the case with Colombia, which keeps its aircraft armed with bombs and rockets this is considered sufficient. In Brazil, the use of machine guns is usually enough to ward off the common threats in the Amazon region. However, in the event of tension escalating and/or conflict, the FAB can keep more aircraft available on the flight line, fuelled and armed with other weapons.

The most common call for the A-29 at the FAB is to intercept unknown or illegal air traffic as in this instance:

'Aircraft intercepted, here is the interceptor. In order to alert you to fulfil Air Defence orders, two warning bursts will be fired.'

The message was clear, but the pilot of the single-engine EMB-721 Sertanejo, Brazilian registration PT-EXP, intercepted by the FAB on 24 October 2015, made a point of ignoring the alert even seeing the tracers from the 12.7 mm (.50in) machine guns of the A-29 crossing the sky at his side.

'Aircraft intercepted, here is the interceptor. If from this moment on the orders of the Brazilian Air Defence are not fulfilled, weapons will be used against your aircraft, which may be damaged or destroyed. Confirm that you are aware and obey the orders of the Air Defence.'

The result of the impact of 12.7mm (0.5in) rounds from Super Tucano machine guns on an EMB-721 Sertanejo. The interceptor opened fire after the pilot refused orders to land.
(Archive João Paulo Moralez)

Twenty minutes later, shots from an A-29 of the 3°/3° GAV were heard, hitting the Sertanejo's wings. Near Japorã, in Mato Grosso do Sul, the aircraft diverted to Paraguay where it crash-landed, being found the following day by that country's authorities. The pilot fled and there was found to be only one seat in the aircraft, allowing more room for the transport of illegal cargoes, such as drugs and weapons. The same aircraft had previously been detained by Paraguayan authorities for smuggling electronics in 2012.

This action was a result of the Destruction Shot Act – or, as it is popularly known in Brazil, the Shoot Down law.

On 17 October 2004, Presidential Decree No. 5,144 came into force in Brazil, regulating Article 303's second paragraph, in Law No. 7,565, of 19 December 1986. In practice, it allowed the FAB to execute the destruction shot with any of its aircraft, something that until then could not be done, with the result that military pilots could execute only warning shots. Drug dealers knew it and took advantage of this limitation to cross the country at will.

Along with the new law, a series of procedures was also adopted to ensure that mistakes were not made and innocent aircraft destroyed. The law includes aircraft suspected of being linked to international arms and drug traffic, without a flight plan, which enter Brazil from regions or countries which are known to produce drugs or serve as a route for their transportation.

When detected by Brazilian radar, air traffic controllers will try to contact the aircraft so that it can be properly identified, especially on routes which are known to be used by drug dealers. If the FAB cannot establish contact or the aircraft refuses to divulge information about route, origin, destination etc., it is classified as suspicious, and measures are progressively triggered.

In 2009, the first firing of a warning shot by the FAB occurred, concerning a single-engine aircraft over the Brazilian border with Bolivia. It was 3 June when an FAB E-99 AEW&C identified the Cessna U206G Station Air, registration number CP-1424, at the suspicious altitude of 91m (300ft) above ground. The E-99 vectored one A-29 to the Cessna, which found a crew not unwilling to cooperate. A change of stance by the Bolivian aircraft occurred after the A-29s fired a warning shot. The Brazilian pilot com-

Night vision googles were planned for the ALX programme from the beginning of its development in the mid-1990s. (IPEV)

municated in Spanish after realising that the aircraft was manned by Bolivians, who made a forced landing and were arrested three days later after a large search operation conducted by the Brazilian Federal Police and the Police of Rondônia. 176kg (388lb) of cocaine were seized from the aircraft.

On Sunday, 25 June 2016, a twin-engine Piper PA-23 Aztec PT-IIJ suffered a total loss after a forced landing in Jussara, Goiás, when an A-29 fired warning shots. From it, 662kg (1,459lb) of cocaine were seized. The damage to drug dealing was USD 4,000,000, which cost the life of the dealer who owned the cargo, as he was summarily executed by those who had ordered the drugs.

Most interceptions are made on the borders of Brazil with Bolivia and Paraguay. Since the Destruction Shot Act came into force the FAB has already conducted more than 2,000 interceptions. Communications between the A-29 and air defence are encrypted and every step of the interception, including warning and destruction shots, is carried out by following passwords and counter-passwords contained within sealed envelopes. Irregular flights, which had once totalled around 4,000 per year, have decreased by an average of 30 to 35 per cent since the law was passed.

These actions are carried out throughout the year, either singly by the squadrons or through major operations to curb international drug dealing, such as the Agate and Ostium operations. According to another 1°/3° GAV A-29 pilot who also asked to remain anonymous:

'During Agatha 1, held in August 2011 in the northern region bordering Colombia, they had two missions attack to clandestine runways. The first one was nocturnal, employing NVGs with four aircraft carrying two BAFG-230 bombs each. A fifth A-29 remained orbiting at high altitude, charged with intelligence, search for enemy presence and damage assessment, equipped with a Star SAFIRE II FLIR, plus an R-99 doing imaging and communications. The same mission was repeated on another runway, but at daytime and with the same amount of aircraft involved. The attack was a success and interdicted the 1,400m (4,593ft) long and 15m (49.2ft) wide runway. The site was not used for four years, a factor evidenced by the presence of secondary vegetation that was taking back the runway'.

It is not necessary for the FAB to use guided bombs with its A-29s. The sight system developed by Embraer is so accurate that errors are up to 5m (16.4ft) from the target, even with the use of NVGs. The United States and countries supported by it, such as Afghanistan and Lebanon, operate with guided bombs where combat occurs near urban centres, so that collateral damage can be kept to a minimum. The same happens in Colombia, in which extensive use of this type of weaponry is made.

FAB fighter pilot specialisation

One of the objectives of the Third Squadrons is the specialisation of the fighter pilots, since it is in these units that they will experience more flight hours and real operational missions. Suffice it to say that while the cost of a flight hour for an A-29 is around USD 1,000, that of an F-5EM is about USD 10,000 and an AMX 12,000 – at least a tenth of the flight cost of a FAB combat jet.

In Super Tucano squadrons the pilots take a huge operational leap. In the first year they receive their IFR cards, enabling them to travel alone with the aircraft across

1°/3° GAV
'Esquadrão Escorpião'
Ala 7, Boa Vista
2005–today
(A-29A and A-29B)

2°/3° GAV 'Esquadrão Grifo'
Ala 6, Porto Velho
2005–today
(A-29A and A-29B)

3°/3° GAV
'Esquadrão Flecha'
Ala 5, Campo Grande
2006–today
(A-29A and A-29B)

Brazil. They also learn to fly with the NVGs, from basic to tactical flights such as formation, attack, interception and others. At the same time they start flying in the No. 3 position, meaning that they become the direct substitute of the leader in a combat situation. They therefore have greater responsibility in planning the mission, in fulfilling the time over the target and in the flight itself, assisting and alerting the leader if any error is made. In the second year these pilots form the leaders of fighter aviation – the pilots who will plan the missions and lead wings and squadrons and they also enter the squadron alert rotation schedule.

It is in those squadrons that the interception training flights intensify. The pilots go through situations where the intercepted aircraft has a radio malfunction or does not want to cooperate and which even involve situations where the intercepted aircraft has dubious intentions.

Although the FAB aircraft are not equipped with chaff/flare, pilots can simulate its use through radio in operational training missions, and FLIR is also widely used in a variety of situations. One such is in the Forward Air Traffic Controller to steer and guide a squadron in an attack, both by night and by day.

Another A-29 pilot who remained anonymous reported that:

'I've already made some interceptions guiding lost aircraft, with navigation system or radio malfunctions. With the datalink we can use voice and data between the A-29, but only voice between other aircraft with datalink and with ground stations. With this system we can send messages, points of interest, coordinates, enemy targets describing what they are (anti-aircraft defence and its range, for example). If connected and synchronised by the datalink, the planes, speeds, altitude and direction are shown on the map of each plane of that squadron.

You can perform a mission using only datalink with complete radio silence, both day and night. With FLIR it is possible to mark the target, pass the coordinates to the other squadron' members and determine which weapons should be used.

We also make so-called Continuous Operations, which last from 24 to 48 hours, involving up to eight aircraft. The objective is to conduct air defence, armed reconnaissance, attack, CAS and other missions, always keeping aircraft in flight in that period. When one squadron lands, the other has already taken off. We get more than 90 per cent of aircraft availability and we flew more than 87 hours in one of those years, for example'.

In addition to the datalink, it is very common for the A-29 to operate in conjunction with FAB's E-99 AEW&C, which in this case, vectors the attack aircraft to intercept another aircraft.

After five years and around 1,200 hours of cumulative flight time, A-29 pilots head to the first-line fighter squadrons, in contact with the higher-performance F-5EM and AMX A-1/A-1M. With the new aircraft pilots will learn to fly on higher performance platforms – with consequent increased G-load on manoeuvres – and with chaff/flare, radar, RWR, use of BVR doctrine, guided weapons and more.

But the whole concept of glass cockpit, instrument panel symbology, NVG use, mission planning/debriefing and datalink will not be new to them. The adaptation to flight is much faster and easier, fulfilling the promise of the Super Tucano that was envisaged during its development in the mid-1990s: to serve as an aircraft which helps the fighter pilot to evolve and to fly fourth generation jet aircraft.

An A-29 four-ship formation lines up for air-to-air gunnery during a training sortie. (Archive 3°/3° GAV)

In-flight testing

The Instituto de Pesquisas e Ensaios em Voo (IPEV, In-Flight Research and Testing Institute), which reports to the Department of Aerospace Science and Technology (DCTA), have replaced the veteran Embraer EMB-326 Xavante attack jets for the instruction of test pilots and test flight engineers at the FAB.

Located in São José dos Campos (SP), IPEV received two A-29Bs – FAB 5923 on 15 March 2012, followed by FAB 5953 in the same year. The second aircraft, however, was lost in an accident on the ground in Gavião Peixoto, Embraer, and was replaced on 26 June 2013 by the A-29B FAB 5924.

At IPEV the Super Tucano also participates in all type of operational testing missions such as the in-flight certification campaign of the towed-target pod installed ventrally in the aircraft. Named NP-AV-1TAS, the system is produced by the Brazilian company Equipaer, weighs 89kg (196lb) and the towed banner – supporting 20mm, 30mm and 50mm calibre impacts – is 10m (32.8ft) long, 1.82m (5.97ft) wide and weighs 12kg (26.4lb). The campaign held in Natal took place from 30 May to 12 June 2016 with several tests and launches in flight, all of which were successful.

The Super Tucano served to test the new telemetry antennas received by the Institute in early 2015, proving its efficiency and receiving and transmitting data to a ground station in real time and at distances of up to 240km (130nm). Also, from 30 October to 3 November 2016, Super Tucano FAB 5924 participated in an in-flight test campaign to certify operation with the 128kg (282lb) BAFG-120 bomb, similar to the Mk 81.

Finally, on 8 December 2015 the Super Tucano won another mission in the IPEV by becoming a platform for the formation of spin tests. Since the departure of the

Instituto de Pesquisa e Ensaios em Voo (IPEV)
Departamento de Ciência e Tecnologia Aeroespacial, São José dos Campos
2012–today (A-29B)

EMB-312 Tucano in 2012, this capacity was lost to IPEV, which was now once again able to reactivate the missions after replacing its old telemetry system and installing test flight instrumentation in the A-29.

To date, the two aircraft in service have flown more than 700 hours each after joining the FAB from other operational squadrons.

New ambassadors for the FAB

Esquadrão de Demonstração Aérea (Esquadrilha da Fumaça)
Academia da Força Aérea, Pirassununga
2012–today
(A-29A and A-29B)

After operating the EMB-312 Tucano for almost 30 years and having made 2,363 demonstrations in Brazil and abroad, mainly in Latin American countries, the US and Europe, on 31 March 2012 the Esquadrão de Demonstração Aérea (EDA, Air Demonstration Squadron) – or Esquadrilha da Fumaça (Smoke Squadron), as the group is popularly known – bade farewell to the Tucano to enter a new era – that of the Super Tucano.

There were several reasons leading the Aeronautic Command to decide to deactivate the Tucano in the EDA. Chief among them was the fact that the fleet was suffering great operational friction due to the high G-load manoeuvres endured both in demonstrations and in training. Not infrequently EDA aircraft were sent to the AFA to train future military pilots, receiving in return airframes with longer life spans and greater resistance to fatigue.

But while analysing this question and the wear and tear of the fleet, it was realised that the AFA would have a low number of aircraft available rather sooner than predicted, with the result of there being insufficient aircraft to continue training its cadets. But, more seriously still, the Tucano might have to be retired earlier than planned.

In addition, one of Fumaça's missions is to reaffirm the capacity of the Brazilian aeronautical industry and to advertise its products around the world. Thus, by adopting the Super Tucano, Fumaça would be promoting the latest product of the Brazilian aeronautical industry.

Preparing for the new aircraft

Almost every year Fumaça says goodbye to pilots, who are replaced by new officers that take positions in the team. Everyone who applies to join the team, from pilots to mechanics and administrative staff, is a volunteer.

For the new aircraft, Fumaça needed three pilots who were instructors in the Super Tucano, so that when new aircraft arrived in the team, they could help to introduce the other members to the new aircraft. Those chosen were Lieutenant Thiago Romeiro Capuchinho (now Captain), whose training in the EMB-312 Tucano began in mid-2012, followed by Captains (now Majors) Daniel Garcia Pereira and Ubirajara Pereira Costa Junior. The latter two began their instructional flights in October 2012.

With its future aircraft Fumaça had no intention of reinventing the wheel. Thus, it was in their interests that the new A-29 instructor pilots should learn to fly in the air demonstrations with the Tucano, later adapting the manoeuvres to the Super Tucano.

And early 2013 the demonstrations began with the new pilots flying the EMB-312. In addition to the crew being prepared it also was necessary to work to provide the new aircraft which the Fumaça would fly from then on. The FAB equipped the team with

four A-29Bs registered FAB 5963 to 5966 and eight A-29As (FAB 5703, 5707, 5710, 5712, 5717, 5719, 5724 and 5734).

EDA aircraft have some differences with other aircraft in the fleet. They do not have HF radios, which reduces their weight by around 40kg (88lb), nor do they have machine guns and ammunition. Embraer developed a 20-litre (5.28 US gallon) oil tank that replaced the ammo boxes, providing 40 litres (10.26 US gallon) in the two wings. The smoke generators were fitted in place of the machine guns.

Internally for the pilot, the aircraft received a 'smoke on' and 'smoke off' notice in its software, showing that the smoke is or is not flowing normally during a demonstration. Also, it indicates negative G, since the team explores inverted flight with more intensity in its demonstrations and training. Finally, the software also allows aircraft to write short phrases in the sky with smoke.

Prior to retirement of the basic Tucano from the Esquadrilha da Fumaça, an EMB-312 Tucano follows an EMB-314 Super Tucano, revealing the significant differences between these two types.
(Sergeant Johnson Barros, FAB)

The A-29 enters the scene

On 1 October 2012, the first pair of A-29Bs, FAB 5964 and 5965, were officially received by Fumaça, still sporting the green and grey operational paint scheme. In January came the next two A-29Bs and the remaining A-29As were received during 2013.

On 3 October 2012, the A-29B made its first 45-minute flight so that Lieutenant-Colonel Esteves, then Commander of Fumaça, could get to know the aircraft, with Captain Marcelo Silva who was not in the EDA, in the rear seat.

During airshows, the Esquadrilha da Fumaça prefers to use the single-seat Super Tucano, but the two-seater can also perform the same manoeuvres.
(Sergeant Batista, FAB)

On 18 December Lieutenant-Colonel Marcelo Gobett Cardoso assumed command of the team, leading the Smoke Squadron for three years during the critical period that saw the deployment of the aircraft.

1 April 2013 marked the start of the A-29 deployment, which was divided into two stages with several phases each including ground school, oriented cockpit instruction, flight simulator, basic formation of the A-29 pilot and converting its pilots to become instructors on the A-29.

In parallel with this, the 25 mechanics, graduates and specialists underwent specific training on the Super Tucano both on the assembly line and in the paint shop of the aircraft at Gavião Peixoto, Embraer. They also went through courses at PAMA-LS and, finally, the ground crews visited the A-29 operators at the FAB in Boa Vista, Campo Grande, Natal and Porto Velho.

Sadly, however, the team suffered a major loss in that period, which resulted in the delay of their demonstration debut. On 12 August 2013 a fatal accident with Captain João Igor Silva Pivovar and Captain Fabrício Carvalho ultimately forced the team to stop the deployment and to review all the steps taken so far.

The flights were suspended for three months before being resumed with pilots making isolated flights and then with two aircraft flying in formation just to maintain proficiency in the aircraft. In the meantime, some upgrades of the A-29 were integrated, such as changing the compensator actuator including relays and other electrical components. Also, on 16 October of that year, three aircraft each received a smoke gen-

erator system. Moreover, the oil used to make the trail of white smoke in the sky was replaced with an ecological, biodegradable type, specifically developed for that purpose. It is the same as used by the Blue Angels of the US Navy.

The Esquadrilha da Fumaça's colourful paint scheme seen over the Rio de Janeiro coast. (Sergeant Batista, FAB)

Back to the air show circuit

In May 2015, the demonstration display was ready and finally, on 3 June, two years and two months after the start of the A-29s implementation, Fumaça performed again during a demonstration as part of the Small Swords ceremony for the cadets' first year at the AFA.

The display changed somewhat with the return of more daring manoeuvres such as the Lancevaque which were adored by the public. With the Tucano, the highest altitude for the manoeuvres is 914m (3,000ft), but this increased to 1,371m (4,500ft) with the Super Tucano. The minimum altitude in the Tucano is 60m (200ft), while in the Super Tucano it is 914m (300ft). The radius of curves increased as well as the speed during the manoeuvres, while the time between them was reduced. On average, pilots reach a G-load of +4 to +5 and -2 to -2.5.

In demonstrations the preference is to use the A-29A, but the two-seat A-29B may be used. However, unlike the Tucano in which the mechanics went along with the pilots for the demonstrations, in the A-29 this is no longer possible.

WORLDWIDE OPERATIONS

AFGHANISTAN

Afghan Air Force (AAF, قوای هوایی افغانستان)

When the USAF finally managed to acquire 20 EMB-314 Super Tucano airframes on 23 February 2013, which would be assembled, tested in-flight and delivered by the Sierra Nevada Corporation (SNC) from its facilities in Jacksonville, FLA, the aircraft's destination was already set. All would be donated to the Afghan Air Force as part of the Light Air Support programme (LAS, see page 71).

The arrival of the Super Tucano would bring enormous benefits to the country. At that time, the Afghan Air Force had no combat fixed-wing aircraft, possessing only helicopters which, in addition to their obsolescence, did not have sufficient firepower or the ability to reach, using penetration bombs with INS/laser guidance, terrorists huddled in caves and hideouts protected by thick rock formations.

While air superiority would be provided by US fighters and the NATO-formed coalition, the country needed to increase counter-insurgency flights and CAS, and the Super Tucano had the perfect ingredients to supply all the country's needs in that war.

The Super Tucano is highly manoeuvrable, with excellent ballistic protection for the crew and the engine and with the possibility of carrying a wide variety of ordnance including smart weapons. Its flight availability is close to 80 per cent, and an hourly flight costs around USD 1,000, or 25 times less than an F/A-18E/F Super Hornet. Furthermore, it can land on short, unpaved runways, operating successfully with lit-

Kabul Air Wing
Hamid Karzai International
Airport, Kabul
2016–today (A-29B)

Ordnance for the Afghan Super Tucano fleet includes GBU-12 laser-guided bombs.
(USAF)

tle infrastructure or ground support and has become the most modern aircraft in the Afghanistan inventory. In all, 30 pilots and 90 mechanics were selected to receive training on the Super Tucano in the US, going on to become instructors on the A-29 in their country, disseminating the knowledge to future pilots and maintainers of the aircraft.

Training and new orders

The theoretical classes, which included flight simulators, began in February 2015, and the following month the first Afghan pilot took off with a Super Tucano accompanied by an instructor from the 81st Fighter Squadron (81st FS), based at Moody AFB and responsible for all this training. The first eight pilots were declared operational on 18 December 2015. Two days later the first four aircraft were loaded onto the MV *Cape Race*, in Norfolk, Virginia. All were equipped with three drop tanks – two underwing and one on the centreline – arriving in Afghanistan for official delivery at Hamid Karzai International Airport in Kabul Air Wing on 15 January 2016. With them the country received BRITE Star II laser designators and sensors, and GBU-12 laser-guided bombs as well as conventional ordnance.

In March 2016, another four aircraft were received, followed by four others in March 2017, which increased the fleet to 12 aircraft. By August 2017, 48 mechanics and 17 pilots were already trained and, on 26 October the USAF placed a new order for six Super Tucanos to be delivered to Afghanistan during 2018. As a result, training at Moody AFB by the 81st FS for more pilots and mechanics was extended to 2020.

In combat

In Afghanistan, Super Tucano missions are concentrated in attack, escort, reconnaissance, CAS, interdiction and surveillance. Having received registrations YA-1401 to 1408 and YA-1509 to 1520, in addition to operating from Kabul the aircraft also operate prominently from Kandahar, Mazar i Sharif and Shindand.

On operational missions, due to the country's large area and long flight times to provide CAS, it is almost mandatory to use two drop tanks, leaving three stations free to carry a combination of bombs and rocket pods. In addition, with the GBU-12, flights are made with two guided bombs and two drop tanks. Mandatorily, aircraft depart for missions with chaff/flare loads.

On 28 February 2016, two Super Tucanos flew to Nangarhar where they became subordinate to the 2016 Silab Corps of the Afghan National Army (ANA). On 7 March 2016, Mazar i Sharif received two aircraft in support of various CAS operations to stabilise the provinces of Balkh and Kunduz.

In April 2016 the Super Tucano saw the first real actions in the Helmand province in CAS missions and for the first time the aircraft began to act in coordination with two MD530 helicopters in most of the operations, thus combining in the same mission the qualities of both fixed-wing and rotary-wing vectors.

In the 24 hours of 14 April 2016, eight Super Tucanos flew 83 missions and accounted for the deaths of 34 insurgents with seven others injured, in support of the 209th Shaheen Corps of ANA, the division responsible for the north-western part of the

country, in the provinces of Balkh and Kunduz. At the same time, in the Lalpur district of Nangarhar, two militants died in a car and another 41 in attacks in the district of Achin. Five, in turn, were killed in an air strike at Khogyani district.

On 19 April, Super Tucanos conducted 83 CAS and attack missions and succeeded in destroying a bomb factory in the Shahwali Kot district of Kandahar, with the participation of ANA's special forces.

In an air strike conducted on 20 April, at least four insurgents died in the town of Tarinkot in Uruzgan. At the site was a 1938 Dshk 12.7mm (0.5in) heavy machine gun.

On 22 April, 24 terrorists were killed, including six loyal to the Islamic State, in attacks coordinated by Super Tucanos and MD530s in the districts of Achin, Mamand Dara and Ghani Khel at the Nangarhar province and in the district of Zurmat at the Paktia province.

On 18 May, two Super Tucanos killed 17 insurgents including two leaders identified as Hamza and Akbar at Kunar province in the Ghaziabad district. Since they had been received in January 2016, the aircraft had, by this time, already completed 260 combat missions.

The most ferocious attack conducted by the Super Tucano in Afghanistan, and perhaps worldwide, was on 9 September 2017 when attacks with the aircraft left 50 Taliban dead in the Barg-e-Matal district of Nurdistan.

During 2016 Super Tucanos made 152 airstrikes over Afghanistan. From January to November 2017 there were 1,100 CAS missions and 4,000 sorties.

Most missions carried out by Afghan A-29s require long-endurance underwing fuel tanks. Despite these, there are still three external hardpoints for armament, plus two internal machine guns.
(USAF)

ANGOLA

Força Aérea Nacional de Angola
(FANA, Angola National Air Force)

In March 2012 the Government of Angola signed a contract valued at USD 94 million for the acquisition of six EMB-314 Super Tucanos. The airframes would incorporate most of the standard items developed by Embraer, including laser rangefinder, cockpit with three liquid crystal CMFDs and more modern software, including a moving map.

Benefiting from the experience of operating 14 EMB-312 Tucanos in combat missions during the Civil War in the late 1990s and then in the intermediate training of future military pilots, Angola decided to use the new Embraer platform on patrol flights, air defence, interception, CAS, armed reconnaissance, attack, interdiction, combat against terrorists, drug dealers and arms' smugglers and, also, for the initial training of their fighter pilots.

The first three aircraft were received in July 2013, at Catumbela Air Base, Benguela.

For armament, the FANA is considering the use of conventional ordnance, guided air-to-ground missiles and heat-seeking air-to-air missiles, but so far no system has been purchased. The aircraft received registrations R-701 to R-706.

Although Angola took advantage of the EMB-312 for COIN missions, the Super Tucano's primary task is to train fighter pilots.
(FANA)

Pilot training

After being rigorously selected to enter fighter aviation, the future combat pilots' training is divided into six phases which comprise 84 flights, totalling 72 flight hours.

In the first phase the initial contact is made in 20 flights of 50 minutes each with an instructor. After the first solo flight, there are two more flights with the instructor followed by five more solos, totalling 23 hours 10 minutes.

The second phase includes a course of aerobatics to understand and learn the evasive and defensive manoeuvres in air combat and/or bombardment situations. There are ten flights of 50 minutes each, including four solo flights together totalling 8 hours 20 minutes.

The third phase comprises VFR navigation flights, low and mid-altitude flights, use of HOTAS, HUD and digital cockpit systems to make the most of the aircraft's navigation systems. In this stage, there are ten flights of 50 minutes each, of which six are solos, again totalling 8 hours 20 minutes.

In the fourth phase the student studies IFR navigation while operating under adverse weather conditions, airport entrances and exits, Non-Directional Beacons (NDB), VOR, ILS and DME waiting procedures. A further six 40-minute flights are made, all accompanied by instructors, totalling four hours of flight.

The penultimate phase covers formation flights, positioning, manoeuvres, VFR navigation, waiting procedures, bombing and aerial combat. The student makes 15 one-hour flights, half of which are solo, in a total of 15 hours.

The sixth and final phase sees the beginning of bombing simulations, target study, correct weapons selection, knowing and understanding the 'head out and hand on' concept, air-to-ground aiming systems study, including CCIP, CCRP, dive toss, gun and manual as well as air combat sighting systems, such as Lead Computing Optical Sight (LCOS) and snap shot. This phase comprises 15 solo flights of 50 minutes each, totalling 12 hours 30 minutes.

As of now, the FANA's Super Tucano fleet has not received any ordnance, but local studies envisage adding conventional and precision-guided bombs. (Rubens Barbosa)

Regimento Aéreo de
Caças Bombardeiros

Esquadra de
Reconhecimento e Ataque
Catumbela Air Base,
Benguela
2013–today (A-29B)

BURKINA FASO

Force Aérienne of Burkina Faso
(FABF, Burkina Faso Air Force)

Burkina Faso was the first nation on the African continent to acquire the Super Tucano, making it the only theoretically effective means of combat in CAS missions, ground attack, reconnaissance, attack, surveillance, patrol and air defence missions. Until September 2012, when the three aircraft which had been purchased by the FABF on 28 March 2011, (at the same time as Angola and Mauritania), arrived in the capital Ouagadougou, the only effective means of combat had been two Mil Mi-35Ms, which, as helicopters, had limited range, firepower and combat support ability.

The aircraft are based at the Escadrille de Chasse in Bobo-Dioulasso and are equipped only with conventional Super Tucano ordnance. Registrations are 1101/XT-MEA, 1102/XT-MEB and 1103/XT-MEC.

However, due to a lack of spare parts, the aircraft are grounded for most of the time and few flights have been made since their entry into service.

Escadrille de Chasse
Base Aérienne 210,
Bobo-Dioulasso
2012–today (A-29B)

Above: Seen in full Burkina Faso markings, Super Tucano BF 1103 is equipped with two LAU-32 seven-tube launchers for 70mm (2.75in) rockets.
(Archive João Paulo Moralez)

Prior to its delivery flight, BF 1103 is seen as XT-MEC at São José dos Campos, Brazil.
(Paulo César Pinheiro, www.pabloaerobrasil.net)

CHILE

Fuerza Aérea de Chile (FACh, Chilean Air Force)

While combat aviation evolved exponentially in Chile with the Lockheed Martin F-16C/D Block 50, the training of its future fighter pilots remained with the analogue design of the obsolete CASA C-101 Aviojet twin-engine jets. Thus, in 2007, the FACh began studies to buy a new aircraft which could take on this mission, leaving C-101 only with the task of providing the student with the characteristics of a jet flight. The choice fell on the Super Tucano and an agreement announced on 28 April 2008 included 12 two-seat versions in a contract worth USD 100 million.

In the Chilean version the aircraft received a third CMFD in the cockpit, besides a synthetic radar symbology very similar to that of the F-16 Block 50/60. In this sense, the presentation and architecture of the Super Tucano's cockpit resembles that of the F-16. So much so, in fact, that a former FACh commander went so far as to declare that the EMB-314 is the best F-16 training aircraft in the world. This is because the student, through the datalink, can synthetically receive a target on the screen as if the Embraer turboprop was equipped with radar, with the same symbology as the US-made fighter. The student is then able to select his weapon and execute his mission following all procedures, with the instructor judging if his action is correct or not. The datalink can receive information from ground radars, from another radar aircraft or from an AEW&C platform.

Another highlight is the entire electronic war suite such as chaff/flare and the RWR among other sensors, all in a synthetic and simulated way.

The Chilean variant does not have chaff/flare launchers but incorporates the laser rangefinder. The agreement included logistical support, training, flight simulator, MPS and Mission Debriefing Station (MDS).

In 2009, six pilots and several Chilean mechanics went to Embraer in São José dos Campos for theoretical training, and then to Gavião Peixoto where they began their practical flight training. The delivery of the first four aircraft took place on 3 November 2009, and they were then transported to Chile with a stop in Asunción, Paraguay, on 21 December.

Grupo de Aviación No. 1
Base Aérea de Los Condores,
Iquique
2009–today (A-29B)

Like Angola, Chile uses its Super Tucanos to train its future fighter pilots. No weapons are used, but the aircraft are equipped with a full synthetic training package that simulates the use of radar and missile launches.
(FACh)

In Chile, most Super Tucano missions are carried out with at least two underwing fuel tanks. (FACh)

Based at Grupo de Aviación No. 1 (Aviation Group No. 1) at Los Condores Air Base in Iquique, they received registrations from 451 to 462 and March, April and May 2010, the remaining aircraft were delivered.

2010 marked the beginning of Chilean operations with the Super Tucano. The training course comprises 100 hours of flight, but the student begins with theoretical instruction, flight simulator before moving on to the practical phase, including VFR, IRF, formation, basic navigation, tactical navigation, low-altitude navigation, air-ground employment and interception with air combat. No weaponry is used in the training missions.

Chile is the only operator using the Super Tucano solely for instruction. In case of conflict or an operational need, the aircraft may use armaments, but this is not a mission yet considered by the FACh. However, this will change with the new purchase of six more Super Tucanos announced in October 2017. The delivery is expected to be completed in 2018 and the purchase aims to reinforce the fleet of Aviation Group No. 1, with new registrations from 463 to 468. Sources say that Chile should start withdrawing its F-5E/F fleet which is currently in Aviation Group No. 12 in Punta Arenas. The aircraft are suffering from great structural fatigue and their flight availability is increasingly impaired. The intention in the future is to replace them with the Super Tucano in the missions of air vigilance and combat air patrol. Geopolitically speaking the main adversary in the region, Argentina, no longer has a combat capability to justify the presence of fighters in the region. Peru, currently the only real threat in the area, can be opposed by the F-16C based in Antofagasta, in the northern part of the country.

COLOMBIA

Fuerza Aérea Colombiana (FAC, Colombian Air Force)

If the EMB-312 Tucano began to pave the way for the defeat of the Colombian Revolutionary Armed Forces (FARC), the EMB-314 certainly brought about the weakening and the demise of the largest and most active guerrilla and terrorism group in Latin America. With Marxist-Leninist indoctrination, the armed movement emerged in 1964 and gained strength over the years with its illegal operations and anti-imperialist stand against the government. The guerrillas conquered and occupied large parts of Colombian territory, reaching 28 of the 33 departments and 282 of 1,102 municipalities.

In September 2002, Colombia was taking its first steps towards purchasing a new aircraft to replace the OV-10 Bronco and A-37 Dragonfly fleets which, despite modernisation and the FACs attention to keep them up-to-date, were already showing signs of obsolescence and low flight availability. The country was looking for a single-engine turboprop that could fly and operate from remote locations with little infrastructure, as at that time there were only 25 runways in the country which could support the operation of jets.

In December 2005 a contract worth USD 235 million was signed with Embraer for 25 two-seater aircraft, a flight simulator, ground equipment and tools, the training of pilots and mechanics with the Brazilian Air Force and spare parts. The aircraft's weapons comprise conventional Super Tucano ordnance, in addition to the Elbit Lizard II bombs with INS/laser guidance and Griffin bombs. The BRITE Star II FLIR provides target designation and has the ability to capture infrared and TV images.

Colombia became the first foreign operator of the Super Tucano and its fleet forms a significant evolutionary step forward when compared to the Brazilian version by having a laser rangefinder with a range of 20km (10.8nm), fitted under the engine air outlet, two chaff/flare launchers with 30 cartridges each and self-sealing fuel tanks. The instrument panel is similar to that of the FAB with two CMFDs, but avionics and software have improvements and upgrades, including a more streamlined moving map displaying rivers, road and terrain contours.

Colombia had considered the possibility of buying the single seat variant as well, due to its greater range, enabling it to remain longer in flight. But as a precaution, a second crew member on board will assist in navigational accuracy and in attack and target analysis, ensuring that when using weapons there will be no civilians present, and that the objective really is a guerrilla target. Legally, a second crew member on board is included as a precaution.

The country also acquired external armoured shields for the aircraft, capable of absorbing 12.7mm (0.5in) hits, which are used in all operational missions.

On 12 December 2005, the first five aircraft of the order were handed over at Embraer's Gavião Peixoto plant.

Registered as FAC 3101 to FAC 3125, sporting an air superiority two-tone grey camouflage and a huge shark mouth on the nose, the aircraft were ferried with mixed crews (Colombians and Embraer pilots) on a 4,800km (2,590nm) route. In 2006 another ten aircraft were delivered and in 2007 the order was completed.

As the first international EMB-314 customer, Colombia has used its fleet in intensive combat missions against rebels and terrorists.
(Andreas Zeitler)

From the outset, Colombia assigned to the Super Tucano missions of strategic attack, interdiction, armed reconnaissance, CAS, escort, and interception and the aircraft was soon distributed to three air units. The first to receive it was Escuadrón de Combate No. 211 'Grifos' (Combat Squadron No. 211 'Griffin'), subordinate to Grupo Aéreo de Combate 21 (Combat Air Group 21), Comando Aéreo de Combate No. 2 (CACOM-2, Combat Air Command No. 2), which also has an EMB-312 Tucano squadron. Based in Apiay, Meta, the unit is responsible for training the country's Super Tucano pilots as well as the FAC's operational combat missions. In CACOM-2 the flight simulator was installed in June 2009.

Then, in January 2007, it was the turn of the Escuadrón de Combate 312 'Drakos' (Combat Squadron 312 'Drakos'), of Grupo Aéreo de Combate 31 (Combat Air Group 1) subordinated to CACOM-3 in Malambo, Barranquilla and, finally, Escuadrón de Combate 611 (Combat Squadron 611), of the Grupo Aéreo de Combate 61 (Combat Air Group 61) which responds to the CACOM-6, in Tres Esquinas, Caquetá, and which has operated aircraft borrowed from the Grifo and Drakos squadrons since January 2009, alongside the EMB-312 Tucano. In 2016, Super Tucanos started to operate also in the Grupo Aéreo del Casanare (Casanare Air Group), in Yopal, Casanare, with two or three aircraft assigned to surveillance and CAS duties.

In Combat

With the Super Tucano, military air operations now have much more navigational precision thanks to the avionics of the aircraft, allowing it to reach the enemy target at exactly the planned time.

But above all, the greatest advantage was the in use of laser-guided bombs with inertial navigation. With an error margin of less than five metres, the Super Tucano could fly as high as 3,048m (10,000ft) without being identified visually or by the sound of the engine. By operating from these altitudes, and with a precise navigation system, the surprise effect of bombing is greatly enhanced.

It was by these means that Colombia succeeded in eliminating one of FARC's leaders, whose death affected the entire financial and economic base of the guerrillas. Tomás Medina Caracas had joined the ranks of the guerrillas, the Frente 16 movement, in 1987. Under his guidance, Frente 16 expanded their war capacity through the profits generated by drug dealing, and at the same time it grew in number of personnel.

With 23 arrest warrants issued against him for the crimes of terrorism, torture, kidnapping, drug dealing and extortion among others, Negro Acácio – as he was popularly known – became a prime target for the Colombian authorities who began to plan various operations to try to capture or kill. In Operación Gato Negro (Operation Black Cat), on 1 February 2001, the action resulted in the arrest of another drug kingpin, Brazilian Fernandinho Beira-Mar, who worked with Negro Acácio smuggling drugs into Brazil.

Because he was a criminal who was wanted by the government and was of great value to the guerrillas, Negro Acácio had considerable protection. He travelled by land several times a day, did not sleep in the same place for more than one night and his camps had distant patrols which created safe boundaries. They were therefore able to fight the Colombian Army and enable the drug dealer to escape and also to warn about the presence of aircraft. From their locations up to 40km (21nm) away, men were constantly on watch. But on the night of 3 September 2007, the fate of Negro Acácio was sealed with Operación Sol Nasciente (Operation Rising Sun). One of the main leaders of the Colombian guerrillas would participate briefly in a meeting which was to begin at 4.30. The operation was attended by the Colombian Army's Rapid Action Forces, which had laser designators aimed towards the bunker located in the heart of the Amazon forest, on the banks of the Guaviare River between San José and Barranco Minas. It was 4.39 when 16 Griffin bombs showered upon the bunker. Negro Acácio and 17 other guerrillas were dead. With this victory a hard blow had been struck against the guerrillas and there was much celebration.

The operation had begun three months earlier. There were four aircraft each equipped with four Israel Aerospace Industries (IAI) Griffin bombs. For navigation they relied on night vision goggles. Apiay, the headquarters of the Escuadrón 211, was approximately 400km (216nm) or one hour's flying time from the camp. The attack began at an altitude of 3,048m (10,000ft).

Unlike those in many air forces, Colombian pilots and ground troops achieve perfect coordination as a result of being trained in increased interaction, communication and understanding between them. Thus, when requesting air support, a troop can pass to the pilot exactly the information he is looking for.

With the success of Operation Rising Sun, Colombia triggered three other important operations with considerable international repercussions. Chief among them was Operation Phoenix, whose objective was to capture or kill FARC number two Luis Édgar Devia, or Raúl Reyes, of the Frente 48 movement. He had escaped five earlier attacks.

Grupo Aéreo de Combate 21

Escuadrón de Combate No. 211 'Grifos'
Apiay, Meta
2005–today (A-29B)

Grupo Aéreo de Combate 31

Escuadrón de Combate 312 'Drakos'
Malambo, Barranquilla
2007–today (A-29B)

**Grupo Aéreo de
Combate 61**

Escuadrón de Combate 611
Tres Esquinas, Caquetá
2009–today (A-29B)

On 1 March 2008 Reyes was in a camp in Granada, in the Putumayo Department, on the border with Ecuador, in the region of Piñuña Blanco. After midnight, Reyes crossed to another camp on the Ecuadorian side, 1,850m (1.14 miles) from the border where there were computers, weapons, USD 39,000, a prisoner and a few other guerrillas.

At 01.30 ten Elbit Lizard 2 bombs dropped from five Super Tucanos hit the camp. The weapons were launched from high altitude, inside Colombian air space, but all hitting Ecuadorian territory. Minutes later, four Black Hawks landed on the spot. They were carrying troops and police officers who performed a quick assessment of the place and confirmed the activities of the operation. Reyes was dead, along with 16 other guerrillas. His body was brought aboard one of the Black Hawks and taken back to Colombia.

All this action resulted in generating a deep sense of unease between the governments of the two countries, since Ecuador was not aware of that secret operation.

On 22 and 23 September 2010 through Operación Sodoma, the target was Victor Julio Suárez Rojas, aka 'Mono Jojoy', another guerrilla leader. With him, 16 militiamen died in a reinforced concrete bunker built under cover of the jungle in La Macarena, at Meta department.

It took more than four years for the Colombian government to discover the site and to develop a detailed intelligence plan for the attack which eventually ended with the death of Mono Jojoy. Bombs from Super Tucanos fell at 01.00 on 22 September in three attack waves to sweep the bunker and these were followed by the deployment of 400 special forces' men who arrived to assess the damage.

There was, however, still one more name left on the hit list. It was Alfonso Cano, FARC's supreme leader. Usually accompanied by a group of people, the leader was in La Vereda del Chirriadero, between the municipalities of Morales and Suárez, in Cauca, on 4 November 2011 when he was killed in an attack by seven aircraft. The attack, Operación Odiseo (Operation Odysseus) lasted less than three minutes. In the ten minutes following the attack, 900 men from the Army and National Police arrived at the site to carry out security and sweep. Along with Cano 'El Zorro', one of the members of his security team, also died and 'El Indio Efraín', his head of security was detained.

But it wasn't all success. The FAC also had losses with the Super Tucano in the fight against the FARC. On 11 July 2012, A-29 FAC 3122 of the Escuadrón de Combate 312 'Drakos' crashed in Cauca during a mission against the FARC some 20km (10.7nm) from Toribio. The aircraft, contrary to what was claimed by the FARC, crashed in consequence of a pilot's error, who, due to bad weather, hit the ground during low-altitude manoeuvres. To this day, no Super Tucano has been brought down after being hit in combat.

The Super Tucano has helped to reduce illegal flights by drug dealers' in Colombia by approximately 95 per cent. It is believed that at the time of writing around five aircraft have been shot down by Super Tucanos, and many clandestine runways have been taken out of operation by interdiction missions carried out by Embraer's aircraft.

In 2011, two CACOM-6 Super Tucano A-29s attacked FARC guerrillas who had entered combat against Sexta División (Sixth Division) forces, leaving two soldiers dead and two wounded in Caquetá.

Aircraft commonly operate prominently from many locations to carry out a wide variety of tasks. This was the case, for example, in February 2016 when two A-29s

**Grupo Aéreo
del Casanare**
Yopal, Casanare
2016–today (A-29B)

of CACOM-2 operated from the headquarters of the Grupo Aéreo del Amazonas (Air Group of the Amazon) in the city of Letícia, on the border with Brazil. The mission consisted of five reconnaissance flights to identify and map illegal gold mining.

Colombia uses both precision-guided bombs and conventional armament in combat missions against guerrillas. This aircraft carries four Mk 82 bombs. (Carlos Lorch, Revista Força Aérea)

Help from outside

Most external aid for Colombia's fight against drug trafficking comes from the United States, and includes training, weapons financing, equipment modernisation, etc. This continuing partnership began in 1992 and, without the US, the war against the FARC would have been far more difficult.

The aim of the FAC is to further increase the issue of interoperability with other forces and countries and Colombia seeks to standardise its procedures based on those of NATO. Since 2011 the country has been working to expand its focus from an internal perspective to a coordinated and joint operation with other countries in real emergency situations and low intensity conflicts. This includes the air force as a whole, from transport aircraft and helicopters to all combat aviation.

The first major multinational exercise in which Colombia participated, and when for the first time, its Super Tucanos flew beyond the border, was Maple Flag 46 in 2013 in Cold Lake, Canada. It took a year of preparation and involved six aircraft which operated for ten days 7,000km (3,780nm) away from their headquarters.

The next exercise was Angel Thunder, at Davis Monthan Air Force Base, Arizona, in which three aircraft were sent to serve as helicopter escorts in search and rescue missions of crews shot down in enemy territory. At that time, the FAC flew 80 hours on 20 missions and had the opportunity to operate for the first time with Joint Termi-

A Colombian Air Force A-29B flies alongside two USAF A-10s during Exercise Green Flag East in August 2016. Four Colombian A-29s and 45 Colombian airmen were at Barksdale Air Force Base, Louisiana, for the joint training exercise. (USAF)

nal Attack Controllers, Joint Forward Observers and Airborne Forward Air Controllers.

Crowning the series of international exercises, was the Green Flag, a multinational exercise which involved for example, doctrines and attack missions coordinating actions with other participant forces on the ground. The exercise focused on the use of doctrines based on the employment of electronic protection and countermeasure systems to extend the survival of the crews in hostile environments. The FAC's participation was with four aircraft in 2016.

With the result obtained in the Maple Flag exercise, Colombia organised its own international Combat Search and Rescue exercise, Angel de los Andes (Angel of the Andes). Held at Río Negro Air Base, the exercise involved Canada, Chile, the Dominican Republic, Ecuador, Jamaica, Mexico, Panama, Peru, the US and lasted eleven days.

The FAC participated in other binational exercises with the Super Tucano which focused on the interception of drug dealers' aircraft. With the Dominican Republic, there have been six editions of the Caribe exercise, in which the air forces of both countries coordinate the interception of illegal traffic in their respective airspace. Sharing intelligence data also helps to combat these flights. In 2012, in the Caribbean air corridor between these countries, 102 illegal flights were registered, but by 2016 that number had been halved.

In 2003 the number had been extremely alarming, with 635 smuggling flights identified in the airspace between Colombia and Panama. The number at the time of writing is 99 per cent smaller. In Caribe VI, Colombia used the Cessna SR-560 electronic intelligence aircraft to support air operations.

Finally, in July 2009 the COLBRA (Colombia-Brazil) exercise was conducted with Brazil. This involved the 2°/3° GAV 'Esquadrão Grifo' and Escuadrón de Combate No. 211 'Grifos'. The aim of the exercise was to conduct interception procedures and improve coordination between the two countries.

DOMINICAN REPUBLIC

Fuerza Aérea de República Dominicana (FAD, Dominican Republic Air Force)

Since the early 2000s the Dominican Republic had demonstrated its interest in acquiring a batch of EMB-314 Super Tucanos, and it was to form a part of one of Embraer's customer portfolios with the acquisition of ten aircraft and another five as purchase options. However, the Central American country announced the option for the turboprop only on 15 February 2007, having signed a contract in December 2008 for eight two-seat versions. Being a very similar version to that operated by the FAB, with two CMFDs in each cockpit and without laser rangefinder and chaff/flare launchers, the aircraft were purchased for almost USD 93.7 million as part of the country's efforts to purge drug dealers' illegal flights. The purchase was supported by the Brazilian government who financed the deal through Banco Nacional de Desenvolvimento Econômico e Social (BNDES, National Bank for Economic and Social Development). Despite being aware that 15 per cent of the cocaine entering the United States came from Central American countries, Washington did nothing to help the Dominican Republic in this fight.

The first two aircraft were delivered in December 2009 and the remaining six in August 2010, receiving registrations 2900 to 2907. The aircraft helped reduce cocaine traffic from 80 tons (176,370lb) to 13 tons (28,660lb) in 2010 and to virtually zero in 2011, when Super Tucano actions prevented 48 tons of cocaine valued at USD 476 million to enter the country.

Dominican EMB-314s have reduced the number of illegal flights smuggling weapons and drugs into the country almost to zero.
(Dax Román)

Escuadrón de Combate
Base Aérea de San Isidro,
Santo Domingo
2009–today (A-29B)

Currently, around ten aircraft each year try to infiltrate Dominican airspace but they are repelled. This is in contrast to 2007 when 200 drug dealers' flights were reported to be flying low over the treetops and carrying cocaine.

Almost all missions are carried out at night, when most illegal flights take place. The crews employ third-generation NVGs and Star SAFIRE II FLIR to locate and intercept drug dealers' aircraft which, if they do not respond to calls to land at an aerodrome indicated by the country's air defence, they can be shot down by the Super Tucanos, who have presidential authorisation for this.

Since 2010 the Dominican Republic has been in a partnership with Colombia which provides specific training for pilots and operators of Ground Control Intercept (GCI). In addition, it runs binational training exercises. The US also joined the partnership, with its Sovereign Skies operation, which supports the Dominican Republic with equipment, training, intelligence, radar networks and with Boeing E-3s carrying out the search, location and vectoring of the FAD's Super Tucanos to intercept illegal flights.

With the intensification of aerial surveillance, drug dealers began to use other routes, including Guatemala, Haiti and Honduras. For the FAD itself, there was a change in doctrine as drug dealers migrated from the air to the sea using high-performance motor-boats to infiltrate the country with drugs. Camouflaged with tarpaulins, the vessels disguised themselves as they sailed in close formation with large merchant ships, so that their routes would not be visible. Even so, with the United States' support, many of them were detected by radar which vectored the aircraft to the scene. Pursuits frequently lasted from two to three hours, most of them ending with success, as was the case on 9 January 2013 when 1,800kg (3,968lb) of cocaine were seized.

Despite this intense search and interception, no aircraft was shot down or motor-boat destroyed and the Super Tucano has helped greatly to police the skies and seas of the Dominican Republic.

Since many of the FAD Super Tucano flights are long endurance, the use of external fuel tanks is obligatory. (USAF)

The maritime patrol and air policing missions employ two underwing drop tanks and the two 12.7mm (0.5in) machine guns. But the Escuadrón de Combate also uses conventional Super Tucano ordnance. The unit, in addition to its operational missions, is responsible for training the country's combat pilots.

ECUADOR

Fuerza Aérea Ecuatoriana (FAE, Ecuadorian Air Force)

In mid-June 2008, Ecuador acquired 24 Super Tucanos through a USD 270 million contract. The aircraft, in Escuadrón de Combate 2313 'Halcones' (Combat Squadron 2313 'Hawks'), Ala de Combate No. 23 (Combat Wing No. 23), would assume a dual function at the FAE, including training of combat pilots and employment in armed reconnaissance, patrol, CAS, escort and attack missions, among others when in conflict.

As a high-technology aircraft whose avionics are superior to anything the FAE had operated so far, instructor pilots from the Strikemaster and A-37B Dragonfly squadrons were chosen to form what would be known as the EMB-314 deployment team at the FAE.

At the time they were purchased for Ecuador, these Super Tucanos were the most advanced variant in the world. Their pilots have access to a complex moving map system with Ground Proximity Warning System (GPWS), which warns of any obstacle appearing in the trajectory of the aircraft. In a country like Ecuador, which has large mountain ranges in much of its territory, this system becomes essential for flight safety, especially on bad-weather days. The system also assists the pilot on flights with NVGs at low altitude, providing extremely precise information. For training missions, the pilot can receive, via datalink from other aircraft or from radar stations on the ground, different types of targets appearing in the CMFD, simulating air, ground and sea objectives. Thus, the student can be trained in radar engagements and use of weapons according to the parameters of each weapons system.

The armament consists of conventional Super Tucano ordnance plus Elbit Lizard II laser-guided bombs and Star SAFIRE III FLIR and BRITE Star II which features a laser designator and an automatic tracking system for moving targets.

There is also a synthetic Super Tucano simulator to help train the future Super Tucano FAE pilots. It will provide training in the use of weapons, navigation, communication, instrument flights, approach, various malfunctions and emergency procedures, among others. Although it does not have a movement platform, a dome of more than 180 degrees of amplitude gives the pilot the sensation of movement in certain manoeuvres.

The first two Super Tucanos from the FAE were transported to Base Aérea Eloy Alfaro in Manta, on the Pacific coast, in January 2010. The aircraft occupy the administrative and operational facilities and the US-built hangars from where, between 1999 and 2009, the Forward Operating Location Manta operated.

However, before the aircraft were received, the Government of Ecuador opted in May 2010 to lower the order to 18 Super Tucanos and use the money saved to buy 12 used Atlas Cheetah C fighters from the stocks of the South African Air Force.

Each of the 18 Super Tucanos was named after 18 of the 24 provinces that make up Ecuador. Thus, FAE 1010 and FAE 1011 bear the names of the provinces of 'Santa Elena' and 'Santo Domingo de los Tsáchilas', respectively. Next, FAE 1012 'Azuay' and 1013 'Bolivar' were incorporated on 5 March; 1014 'Cañar' and 1015 'Carchi', on 16 April; 1016 'Chimborazo' and 1017 'Cotopaxi' on 21 May; 1018 'El Oro' and '1019' Esmeraldas, on 18 June; 1020 'Galapagos' and 1021 'Guayas', on 12 July; 1022 'Imbabura' and 1023

Ala de Combate No. 23

Escuadrón de Combate 2313 'Halcones'
Base Aérea Eloy Alfaro, Manta
2010–today (A-29B)

Ecuadorian EMB-314s have a dual mission: training future fighter pilots and patrolling the skies.
(João Paulo Moralez)

'Loja', on 7 October; 1024 'Los Rios' and 1025 'Manabí', on 10 December; 1026 'Morona Santiago' on 12 January 2011 and finally, the 1027 'Napo' on 8 April, 2011.

At the start of operations, seven to eight aircraft were kept on the flight line, plus six or seven in the hangar in flying condition.

Students began planning flights using the MPS, where they input information of route, distance to target, the quantity of fuel on board, weaponry to be used, different flight altitudes and points on the route where there are enemy radars and threats, among others.

In addition to training missions, the FAE has two aircraft deployed at Lago Agrio, a base in the middle of the Amazon jungle, to carry out patrol flights, reconnaissance, air policing and interception of aircraft operated illegally by arms and drug dealers. Each aircraft is equipped with two underwing drop tanks, 250 rounds of 12.7mm (.50in) ammunition for each machine gun and, in addition, one of them has FLIR. Suspicious aircraft without a flight plan are intercepted, their origin verified and, on some occasions, the crews of the Super Tucanos order them to land to be checked by a ground crew. In August 2017, as part of Operación Triton, a Super Tucano operating with FLIR located a vessel carrying a ton of cocaine.

Left:
An Ecuadorian pilot adjusts his NVGs before a night sortie.
(João Paulo Moralez)

Right:
Although non-moving, the flight simulator allows the pilot to fly over Ecuadorian terrain and to carry out emergency procedures.
(Santiago Rivas)

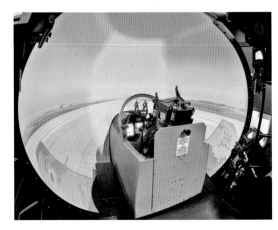

INDONESIA

Tentara Nasional Indonesia-Angkatan Udara (TNI-AU, Indonesian Air Force)

Geophysically, Indonesia is similar to the Brazilian Amazon, with a hot and humid environment typical of an equatorial and mountainous climate which covers almost the entire country.

But by 2005, the OV-10 Bronco fleet did not allow the country any kind of action against a low-intensity conflict or even an intervention. After extensive research and analysis of several aircraft types, the EMB-314 was selected with the country acquiring eight examples on 9 June 2011, and then expanding its fleet to 16 aircraft plus a flight simulator in a contract signed in July 2012. The first four aircraft were delivered in August 2012 along with the flight simulator.

Months after it entered service, Indonesia began to develop capabilities which were previously not possible with the Bronco. Chief of these was a superior gain in manoeuvrability in air-to-air missions. The use of the datalink and the symbology presented through the cockpit screens also proved to be of critical value.

Skadron Udara 21
Abdul Rachman Saleh
Air Base, Malang
2012–today (A-29B)

The main missions of the squadron are against insurgency, armed reconnaissance, escort, attack, interception and patrol. But it is also responsible for training its own combat aviation pilots and teaching all modern doctrines. Pilots of supersonic fighter aircraft, however, follow another route and instead use the KAI T-50.

Indonesia's Tucanos are not yet equipped with conventional or infrared imaging sensors, nor are they fitted with laser-guided bombs, only conventional Super Tucano ordnance.

Registered from TT-3101 to TT-3116, missions are always carried out with at least one ventral drop tank installed for medium-duration missions or two underwing tanks for longer flights.

Beside air patrols, some of which are flown from remote airfields, the TNI-AU's EMB-314s have a secondary attack and COIN role as seen here with a payload of 120kg (264lb) Mk 81 bombs. (Detikom via Pit Weinert)

LEBANON

Al Quwwat al-Jawwiya al-Lubnaniyya (LAF, Lebanese Air Force)

7th Squadron
Hamat Air Base, Batroun
2017–today (A-29B)

A Lebanese Air Force EMB-314 while conducting training in the US.
(USAF)

Since the end of the Lebanese Civil War, which lasted from 1975 to 1990, this tiny country between Syria and Israel has faced varying degrees of instability in many regions, usually as result of religious disputes or terrorist action.

It is the only nation in the Middle East without extensive areas of desert, is culturally Westernised and has a highly developed and globalised structure in comparison with other Arab countries. It is a democracy with 18 religious groups, living in a territory of only 10,452 km² (4,036 sq. miles) and has an estimated population of just over 7.75 million, of which 2.5 million, or around a third of the total, are refugees.

None of this is conducive to the country's stability and the fact that its main religions define the country's politics exacerbates the situation. To further destabilise this delicate balance, although highly professional, the Lebanese Army has many shortcomings in terms of military equipment, for example, the lack of aircraft to provide the air support necessary for the actions of ground forces.

However, in June of 2015, the US government approved the sale of six Super Tucanos to Lebanon, including spare parts, pilot and mechanic training, ground support tools and equipment, two extra engines and 2,000 laser-guided Advanced Precision Kill Weapons System (APKWS) rockets. The sale was officially announced on 8 November 2015 and the country could now have a modern fixed-wing aircraft for CAS missions.

Manufactured by SNC these were the most modern Super Tucanos in operation in the world, superior even to those in Afghanistan. In all, 22 mechanics and 12 pilots were sent to USAF's Moody AFB in early 2017, thus beginning the Super Tucano training that was given by the 81st FS. It consisted of a few weeks of theoretical training, with the first flight by a Lebanese pilot taking place on 22 March 2017. The course lasted a total of seven and a half months, with aircraft transferred to Lebanon in early October, and being fully incorporated by the end of the month.

Destined for the 7th Squadron, the aircraft were registered L-711 to L-716 and due to the country's small size would not need external fuel tanks. From Hamat aircraft can reach the most southerly point of the country in under 30 minutes. The capital Beirut can be overflown by the aircraft in ten minutes, while Tripoli, an area prone to instability, in less than five minutes. The eastern border in the Bekaa Valley is a 13-minute flight.

The aircraft are expected to use conventional Super Tucano ordnance plus the BRITE Star II infrared imaging system and 113kg (250lb) GBU-58 Paveway II bombs.

For Lebanon, a vast operational gap has been filled by the Super Tucano, since attack and CAS missions are of major significance today and are therefore demanded by the country. With the new turboprops, emergency situations can be solved quickly, thus providing the much-desired sovereignty on internal security.

REPUBLIC OF MALI

Force Aérienne de la Republique du Mali (FARM, Republic of Mali Air Force)

Mali's biggest internal security problem is the ultra-violent and radical al Qaeda of the Islamic Maghreb (AQIM) terrorist group. Working in partnership with Mauritania, where troops of both countries can cross each of their borders in search of terrorists and smugglers, Mali also opted for the Super Tucano, adopting the same aircraft and a similar configuration to that of their friendly neighbour.

On 15 June 2015, Embraer announced the contract with the country for six units equipped with external ballistic protection for up to 12.7mm (0.5in) impacts on the cockpit and engine.

In its choice of armaments, the FARM can choose from the range of conventional Super Tucano ordnance. Because it is a large country, missions in Mali must be undertaken with two underwing fuel tanks, but this still leaves three hardpoints free for weapons.

The six Malian aircraft were financed through BNDES, but as the country did not provide the necessary guarantees for payment of its aircraft, the order was reduced to four. At the time of writing the aircraft were ready to be delivered and it was expected that they would be ferried to the customer in 2018.

Base Aérienne 102 in Sévaré, located in the centre of the country, will host the squadron in order to be closer to the conflict zone threatened by the terrorist group AQIM. Due to the presence of terrorists, Mali is generally unstable and its Super Tucanos will be required primary to conduct combat missions including ground attack, reconnaissance, patrol, CAS and air defence. They will also be used for training combat pilots.

Escadrille de chasse
Base Aérienne 102, Sévaré
Expected 2018 (A-29B)

Although still to be delivered, Mali's EMB-314 fleet is one of the few equipped with external armour plates.
(Rubens Barbosa)

MAURITANIA

Force Aérienne Islamique de Mauritanie (FAIM, Islamic Air Force of Mauritania)

Super Tucano Squadron
Base Aérienne 210, Atar
2012–today (A-29B)

Of all the African operators of the EMB-314 Super Tucano, Mauritania's fleet is the one most actively employed in combat missions.

In March 2012, Embraer announced the sale of two examples to Mauritania, which were delivered in October of that year by Embraer and Mauritania pilots. Their registrations were 5T-MAU and 5T-MAW.

Super Tucano is used mainly at night, using NVGs, and almost always in coordination with Mauritanian special forces on the ground. Most of the operations occur in the north-east and east of the country, on the borders with Mali and Algeria, the most sensitive regions of the country.

In a vast country where 80 per cent of the land surface is desert, the missions are always long lasting, typically of around six hours in the air, reaching targets 1,110km (600nm) from the base and remaining 30 minutes over the target. For these missions the aircraft take off with three external fuel tanks. Fighting is mostly against lightly armoured vehicles or even pick-ups equipped with barrel weapons, and in those situations the Super Tucano employs two 12.7mm (.50in) machine guns and two seven-shot 70mm (2.75in) LAU-32 rocket pods.

The FAIM Super Tucanos carry out extensive work of search, pursuit and attack against terrorists in desert areas.

With help of special forces on dark, moonless nights, soldiers illuminate the targets with a laser designator and the Super Tucano attacks at the ends of the beam line or near it using third generation NVGs. With each attack the aircraft makes a damage assessment in coordination with the troops, who can request further attacks if required.

If the night is clear, the pilots employ NVGs for the attacks, without the assistance of ground troops.

Since 2011, mainly due to the Civil War in Libya, the Mauritanian Army has found several 9K32 Strela-2 (SA-7) MANPADS in the hands of the AQIM terrorists and, bearing this in mind, their aircraft always use chaff/flare cartridges for self-protection.

The navigation for the missions is adopted in the Hi-Lo-Hi profile with the aircraft climbing to above 3,570m (12,000ft), but in higher risk actions aircraft can adopt Lo-Lo-Lo navigation while maintaining the mission's surprise effect.

These actions are also part of Operation Enduring Freedom – Trans Sahara, conducted by the US with the participation of Germany, Canada, Spain, France, the Netherlands and the United Kingdom, supporting countries including Algeria, Burkina Faso, Chad, Mali, Mauritania, Morocco, Niger, Nigeria, Senegal and Tunisia with training and equipment. Through intelligence, combined operations, access to equipment and training, the aim of the operation is to dismantle extremist terrorist groups, smugglers and drug dealers operating in the region, mainly al-Qaeda.

On 24 September 2017, five drug dealers were arrested with a ton of drugs in the El Hank area, bordering Algeria, in the far north of the country. Their Toyota vehicle was

detected by a Super Tucano who shot at the engine to force the vehicle to stop. It then led troops on the ground to carry out their arrest. The dealers carried pistols, large quantities of ammunition, machine guns and rifles, plus a satellite phone.

The day before, a Super Tucano also intervened against miners who were illegally extracting gold in the country.

In addition to combat missions in Mauritania, the Super Tucanos are also used to train future combat pilots. The country has placed a new order for two more aircraft to be delivered in 2018.

Missions in Mauritania have an endurance of up to 6.5 hours, making the use of three external fuel tanks obligatory. Most sorties rely on machine guns against terrorists in pick-up trucks, as bombs have been found to have little to no effect in this kind of conflict. (FAIM)

PHILIPPINES

Hukbong Himpapawid ng Pilipinas (PAF, Philippine Air Force – PAF)

The latest operator of the Super Tucano is the Philippine Air Force, which has acquired six examples in December 2017. For years, the country had flirted with Embraer's counter-insurgency aircraft and with scenarios and geography very similar to those of Brazil in regard to tropical weather, dense forests, high temperatures and humidity, there would be no problem for an Embraer platform to adapt to its operational environment. Also in 2017, not for the first time, the country suffered from problems with its domestic security when Maute rebels and terrorists supported by the Islamic State occupied the city of Marawi, in Mindanao. The air force mobilised its combat capability, including the FA-50, OV-10 Bronco, AW109, SF260 and Bell UH-1 while naval aviation operated its AW109, Bo 105, Islander and UAVs on surveillance missions. It is possible these last actions accelerated the decision to order a modern CAS aircraft.

Little is known about the systems, armaments and other equipment that will be part of the Philippines' Super Tucano fleet. However, aircraft will be based with the 15th Strike Wing, located at Danilo Atienza Air Base which has five combat squadrons comprising the 16th Attack 'Eagles' Squadron flying the OV-10, the 17th Attack 'Jaguars' Squadron with the SF260TP, the 18th Attack 'Falcons' Squadron operating the AW109E Power, the 19th Composite Tactical Training 'Griffins' Squadron and the 20th Attack 'Firebirds' Squadron with the MD520MG Defender.

Delivery is expected to start in 2019.

15th Strike Wing
Danilo Atienza Air Base,
Cavite
Expected 2019 (A-29B)

UNITED STATES

United States Navy (USN), United States Air Force (USAF) and private owners

The first 'official' US contact with the Super Tucano was at the end of February 2008, with the lease of the EMB-314 c/n 31400082 to its first private operator, EP Aviation LLP, a subsidiary of the notorious and controversial security company Blackwater.

Wearing the registration N314TG, the two-seat aircraft was given the initial mission to participate in the USN Imminent Fury programme. The objective was to analyse a platform with a low cost of acquisition and operation, but capable of flying in the most aggressive environments, with minimal infrastructure, taking off from unprepared runways or highways and being technologically similar to fourth generation fighters.

The plan was to provide more support for special operations forces such as the Navy SEALs and at the same time ensure greater independence from USAF's Fairchild A-10 Thunderbolt II which, despite being adored by the SEALs, were so overburdened that they couldn't always could respond to navy calls.

The Super Tucano, despite not carrying the same weapon load and having less protection for its crew and systems than the A-10, was a viable option in terms of acquisition and operation costs, and would be much more efficient in the intended mission than the navy's inventory jets. Compared to the F/A-18 and F-35, where per-hour flight costs are estimated at USD 25,000 and USD 39,000 respectively, the Super Tucano performed the same attack mission using the same weaponry, with greater efficiency and flexibility for USD 1,000 an hour.

Thus, the N314TG was extensively improved by receiving new communication, navigation and weapons systems, modifications which were conducted in Patuxent River NAS, Maryland, and which also included Link 16, satellite communications and the SecNet 54 wireless internet encryption system. Only then did the aircraft begin a series of tests using Star SAFIRE III EO/IR sensors, Star SAFIRE HD and BRITE Star II and conventional armament such bombs and rockets. Air to ground gunnery was facilitated using the two Super Tucano's machine guns.

Phase I of Imminent Fury least lasted for a year, was successfully completed and the trials continued with the lease of three other aircraft which would be sent to theatres of operation, where they could be tested in a real combat environment. However, all work was stopped.

The N314TG was transferred to Xe Aviation LLC, the new name of the Blackwater subsidiary, that was itself renamed Xe, on 22 May 2010. It was then sold to Tactical Air Support Inc. on 30 November 2012 and on 17 May 2017 it passed into the hands of Sierra Nevada Corporation (SNC).

Light Air Support

The Afghanistan and Iraq wars, which began in 2001 and 2003 respectively, were the longest lasting conflicts involving the US since the end of the Cold War.

To cope with the guerrilla movements, terrorism, and localised actions of a non-uniformed, undefined enemy using conventional weapons, the US used an expensive and sophisticated arsenal largely developed during the Cold War, when the price of buying and operating such weapons was not in itself the greatest concern.

However, with the arrival of the new century came a new and challenging reality. Sustaining attacks, CAS, and combat patrols against an enemy entrenched in caves no longer made sense if using the most modern combat of aircraft.

The ability to switch platforms on strike missions by considerably reducing the cost of flight time attracted the USAF's attention. Thus, on 27 July 2009, within the programme called Light Attack/Armed Reconnaissance (LAAR), the Directory of Capability Integration, responding to the USAF Aeronautical Systems Centre, issued a Request for Information for the purchase of up to 100 aircraft which could perform CAS, attack, reconnaissance and escort flights. This impressive number was later reduced to 15, with which the USAF would create a new wing to develop doctrines and tactics and to train USAF pilots to instruct foreign pilots, but without its use in combat. The USAF was considering buying combat aircraft to create a combat capability through the OA-X programme that may reach 176 COIN aircraft for combat use. On the other hand, through the Light Air Support (LAS) programme, at least 20 COIN aircraft could be bought to donate to nations which need to counter terrorism, with Afghanistan and Lebanon on the top of the list. LAAR was eventually cancelled in February 2012.

The LAS became operative on 9 September 2009. The aircraft should have low acquisition and operating costs, be easy to maintain and require little ground infrastructure.

On 26 and 27 January 2010, two Super Tucanos flew to Kirtland AFB in New Mexico to participate in a series of demonstrations. One of the aircraft used in the tests was an example manufactured for Burkina Faso, which at that time was bearing the PT-ZNE civil registration, while accompanying it was a FAB airframe, the A-29B FAB 5951.

On 1 November 2011 the AT-6B was excluded from the programme. On 22 December the same year, SNC, which would be responsible for the assembly, flight tests, deliveries and support of the Super Tucano to the USAF, signed a contract worth

EMB-314 N314TG was used during test and evaluation for the US Navy and also to provide advanced training for certain private companies. Here, the aircraft is seen in Tactical Air Support Inc. colours.
(Andreas Zeitler)

USD 355 million with Embraer for 20 EMB-314s plus a flight simulator, tooling and ground training systems for future pilots.

On 30 December the announcement was made official by the Pentagon, although Beechcraft was struggling to reverse the situation.

The company had been notified that it had not won the competition through a letter issued by the USAF and sent by email on 1 November 2011. But due to technical problems alleged by Beechcraft, the company said it was not aware of the letter until eleven days later, causing it to miss the deadline for appealing the USAF's decision. The Government Accountability Office (GAO) rejected the Beechcraft protest after which the company initiated a series of political manoeuvres, including an appeal to the country's Federal Court. In January 2012, the process was halted, and on 28 February 2012 the USAF itself, alleging problems with documentation that assured Embraer's victory, chose to cancel the LAS and reopen the competition.

The Request for Proposal for the new competition was opened on 5 May with the deadline to submit bids on 4 June 2012. The expectation was to receive the aircraft in the second half of 2014 and on 23 February 2013 the Super Tucano was again elected the winner. The value of the contract rose to USD 427 million for 20 aircraft. Embraer renewed a ten-year lease on land at Jacksonville International Airport where the Super Tucano assembly line was built, generating 1,400 direct jobs. Altogether, 72 per cent of the components of the USAF version originate in the United States. The remainder are the British ejection seats and the Canadian engine.

Beechcraft again tried to challenge the USAF's decision, but this time its move was unsuccessful.

The roll-out of the first Super Tucano produced in the US, registered 13-2001, took place on 25 September 2014. In October 2017, after which six more new Super Tucanos were ordered for the Afghan Air Force. Adding to the Lebanese order and the replacement of an Afghan A-29B lost in an accident with US pilots during a training sortie, the SNC now has orders for 33 Super Tucanos.

Operations with the USAF

On 26 September 2014, the first Super Tucano landed at Moody AFB in Georgia, and on 15 January 2015 the 81st Fighter Squadron was re-activated in the USAF to become the Super Tucano operator in that country. The squadron was appointed to train future Afghan combat pilots and mechanics to operate the Super Tucano fleet in combat in their own country.

Instruction missions were primarily focused on attack, CAS, escort for ground convoys or in-flight helicopters, and armed reconnaissance.

After the theoretical classes and five simulator flights, students began Initial Qualification Training (IQT), which basically taught students to fly the aircraft and use their systems. Training was also given for formation flights as well as for basic manoeuvres, aerobatics, ILS flights etc. In Mission Qualification Training the student learned to use the Super Tucano's guns, which for Afghanistan are seven-shot 70mm (2.75in) LAU-32 rocket pods, Mk 82 conventional bombs, wing machine guns and laser-guided GBU-12 bombs. The student also learned tactical formations and low altitude navigation, among other disciplines.

Blackwater
EP Aviation LLP
McLean, Virginia
2002–2009 (A-29B)

Tactical Air Support, Inc.
Reno, Nevada
2012–2017 (A-29B)

Sierra Nevada Corporation
Sparks, Nevada
2017–today (A-29B)

81st Fighter Squadron
Moody Air Force Base,
Georgia
2015–today (A-29B)

A fully loaded A-29 from the 81st Fighter Squadron. Registered as 13-2002, this aircraft was delivered to the Afghan Air Force in January 2016.
(Neil Dunridge)

The USAF currently supports only the training of nations which are buying the Super Tucano through the Sierra Nevada Corporation. Nevertheless, through the OA-X programme the EMB-314 may even become a combat platform in the USAF inventory (see also Chapter 4).

OA-X, A POSSIBLE REPLACEMENT FOR THE A-10

Even before the USN, the USAF looked forward in 2007 to a new, cheaper and more efficient platform in the COIN mission to fight in the popularly known 'War on Terror'.

Slower than an F-16, flying lower than an A-10 and with a lower weapons-carrying capability, but at a much lower cost, the new aircraft could solve a problem which the air force had been constantly debating over recent years – the fate of its A-10 fleet.

Following the success of the Super Tucano in Afghanistan, Brazil, Colombia, the Dominican Republic and Mauritania, for example, and as its own pilots had already developed an operation doctrine in combat and in irregular warfare, as well the LAS experience when it had the chance to evaluate this type of aircraft, the USAF began the OA-X (Observation and Attack) experiment in 2017. At the same time, the air force also started a new way of evaluating future aircraft to comprise an attack, reconnaissance, CAS, escort and surveillance squadron.

Through a memorandum issued on 8 March 2017 by the Air Force Strategic Development Planning and Experimentation Office, based at Wright-Patterson AFB, it invited the aircraft industry to participate in a campaign to analyse aircraft which could increase its light attack capability.

After setting some criteria and an analysis programme, on 9 August four aircraft arrived at Holloman AFB, New Mexico, to demonstrate their capabilities. These were

EMB-314 PT-ZNV, an Embraer demonstrator, has been used in tests and evaluations for the OA-X programme. This may result in orders for up to 300 aircraft for COIN missions in low-intensity conflicts. (USAF)

In the OA-X programme, the main rival to the EMB-314 is the Beechcraft AT-6B Wolverine. The Brazilian turboprop has the advantage of having been primarily developed for attack missions. The AT-6B, was adapted from a trainer airframe. (Ethan D. Wagner, USAF)

the AT-802L Longsword from Air Tractor and L3, Embraer and SNC EMB-314 Super Tucano, the Scorpion attack jet and the AT-6 Wolverine, both from Textron.

For five weeks each aircraft took off two to three times a day to help the USAF achieve some objectives: to demonstrate the system's ability to find, fix, track and target; to demonstrate datalink interoperability and weapons delivery and accuracy; to demonstrate flight manual predictions and ensure they are accurate to the aircraft's performance; to demonstrate the flying and handling qualities; to demonstrate the systems' functionality; to observe the aircraft's suitability; to observe the aircraft's functionality and to determine the visual platform and aero acoustic signatures.

American crews of the 704th Test Group and 586th Flight Test Squadron carried out the tests, under the demonstration called Combat Dragon III, or Capability Assessment of Non-Developmental Light Attack Platforms.

Since retiring the Douglas A-1 Skyraider in late 1960s, the USAF has never had a single-engine propeller aircraft developed specifically for this type of mission. It is as if the air force itself was rediscovering this type of aviation – but with the addition of everything that technology can provide.

Reports indicate that Embraer mechanics in certain tests were able to replace components such as modules and batteries using simple tools that fit in a hand toolbox, after landing on an unpaved runway at Cannon AFB. This flexibility had a positive effect on the US military who envisioned their operations on highways or landing strips near the battle line with the enemy. By consuming little fuel, few logistics infrastructure would be needed.

The expectation is that up to 300 airframes are purchased, totalling USD 1.2 billion.

It is worth remembering that at the end of July 2017 the USAF stated that it would also evaluate the aircraft from the perspective of US Special Operations Command, called Light Attack Support for Special Operations (LASSO). While OA-X sought to evaluate aircraft performance, LASSO analysed the systems that can be installed on light-attack aircraft to support special operations.

EMB-314 PT-ZNV has been tested in various situations and with a wide range of conventional and precision-guided weapons. (USAF)

APPENDIX I: TECHNICAL DATA

EMBRAER EMB-314 SUPER TUCANO

Manufacturer, programme and prototype

The aircraft was designed by Embraer at São José dos Campos (SP). Embraer's Technical Director, who was also the engineer in charge of the project's coordination was Sérgio Horta and the programme began in January 1991. Embraer's objective was to participate in a North American contest for the Joint Primary Aircraft Training System (JPATS). The inaugural flight of the PT-ZTW, a Proof of Concept airframe based on the structure of the EMB-312 Tucano, took place on 9 September 1991, with test pilot Gilberto Schittini and flight test engineer Mauro César Mezzacappa.

It was then transformed into the ALX programme with two prototypes – PP-ZTV and PP-ZTF. There were three more pre-production prototypes YA-29 5700 and YA-29 5701 (single-seat), and YAT-29 5900 (two-seat).

Production

The Super Tucano is produced at Gavião Peixoto (SP), Brazil. Since 2014, the Sierra Nevada Corporation (SNC) has also operated a production line at Jacksonville, Florida, US, for the Light Air Support (LAS) programme.

A total of one Proof of Concept airframe, five prototypes, three pre-production aircraft and 244 examples have been produced or are in production.

One of the prototypes was destined for the JPATS programme, the other two for the ALX programme and one demonstrator was used by Embraer (PT-ZNV).

The countries operating the Super Tucano and their numbers of aircraft are as follows: Afghanistan (26 in production, one lost in accident which will be replaced), Angola (six aircraft delivered), Brazil (33 single-seaters and 66 two-seaters delivered, ten losses), Burkina Faso (three delivered), Chile (18, 12 delivered), Colombia (25 delivered, one lost), Dominican Republic (eight delivered), Ecuador (18 delivered, one lost), Indonesia (16 delivered, one lost), Lebanon (six, two delivered, four in production), Mali (six, but only four to be delivered at the time of writing), Mauritania (four, two delivered), Philippines (six, to be delivered in 2019), US (one delivered and owned by the Sierra Nevada Corporation).

Role

Advanced trainer, fighter pilot training, attack, fighter, escort, air defence, close air support, intelligence and reconnaissance.

Crew

One or two, depending of the variant. Solo flights are made with the pilot occupying the front position in the cockpit.

Airframe and systems

The windshield can resist bird impacts of 1.8kg (4lb) at speeds of 500km/h (270kts). The structure supports a G-load factor of +7/-3.5 without external load but with external load this is limited to +3.5/-1.8G. Fatigue life is at least 12,000 flight hours in combat but can reach 18,700 flight hours in training. The luggage compartment can carry 40kg (88lb) in the single-seat variant and 10kg (22lb) in the two-seater with two pilots.

The fuselage is of the semi-monocoque type, mainly of aluminium alloy, with a ventral aerodynamic brake and with mechanically or chemically machined coatings. Some revetments are made from glass-, carbon- and Kevlar-reinforced plastics. Two semi wings are attached to the fuselage. The right-hand wing contains one 330 litre (87.17 US gal) fuel tank and there is one 326 litre (86.12 US gal) in the left hand wing. The single-seat variant also has a 304 litre (80.30 US gal) fuselage fuel tank, located in the rear seat nacelle. Each wing fuel tank has a mechanical fuel quantity checking system.

The canopy has an explosive cord to allow access to the cockpit in case of an emergency on the ground and the cockpit is pressurised to 5psi (0.34bar), with Martin-Baker Mk BR10LCX, that provides for ejection at zero altitude and zero speed, the seats adopting divergent trajectories when ejected – the front seat moves to the right and the rear seat to the left. The canopy's explosive cord also weakens the Plexiglas and allows the ejection of the seat through it.

Equipped with OBOGS, HOTAS and air conditioning, the cockpit is compatible with NVGs operation and the front nacelle is equipped with HUD (its data can be viewed in a CMFD in the rear nacelle). Retractable tricycle landing gear is fitted, with or without anti-skid and the wheels stay uncovered when retracted into the wing. The front landing gear can be angled 20 degrees to each side via the pilot's pedals in the cockpit. The tyres are Goodyear Flight Eagle models, the front (nose) being a 17.5x5.75-8 with pressure of 126psi (8.68bar) and the main tyres are 6.5-10s inflated to 134psi (9.24bar).

A de-icing system is installed for the windshield, propeller, pitot and static port. An interception light installed on the engine cover, on the right-hand side, allows the pilot to see the registration of another aircraft in flight when it is between 70m (230ft) and 100m (328ft) away. The aircraft has an auto rudder to assist take-off and for self-defence, two chaff/flare dispensers are fitted, each with 30 cartridges.

Powerplant

The Super Tucano uses a Pratt & Whitney PT6A-68C of 1,600shp (2,000rpm) power plant driving a Hartzell constant pitch five-blade propeller, model HC-B5MA-2/M9128NSK, 2,38m (7,80ft). It can produce a maximum power of 1,250shp with 2,000rpm according to temperature and altitude. These same values apply, according to temperature and altitude, to the maximum normal take-off power allowed and the maximum power allowed during a normal cruising flight.

Dimensions

Wingspan 11.13m (36.51ft), length 11.34m (37.20ft), height 3.97m (13.02ft), wing area 19.40m² (208.8 sq. ft), tailplane span 4.66m (15.28ft), wheelbase 3.35m (10.99ft), wheel track 3.77m (12.36ft). Static propeller clearance from the ground is 38cm (15in).

Weights

Basic weight 3,020kg (6,57lb, single-seat) and 3,110kg (6,856lb, two-seat), maximum take-off weight 5,400kg (11,904lb), maximum landing weight 4,000kg (8,818lb).

Performance

Operating environment from -45°C (-49°F) to + 50°C (122°F), service ceiling 10,668m (35,000ft), stall speed 166km/h (90kts), maximum landing gear operating speed and extended landing gear 277km/h (150kts), maximum speed with flap extended 333km/h (180kts), top speed at sea level 518km/h (280kts), maximum speed 592km/h (320kts), speed for rotate during take-off 166km/h (90kts), maximum autonomy with internal fuel 3.5 hours, maximum autonomy for ferry flight 8.4 hours, maximum ferry range 3,055km (1,650nm), take-off distance to clear 15,24m (50ft) obstacle 900m (2,952ft), landing distance to clear 15.24m (50ft) obstacle 860m (2,821ft). Rate of climb at sea level 988m/min (3,242ft/min), time to climb to 6,096m (20,000ft) 8.3min, inverted flight time is 60 seconds, flying vertically with nose up 15 seconds.

Avionics

Two CMFD 15.24x20.32cm (6x8in) are fitted in each cockpit panel, or a CMFD with 13.76x17.52cm (5.42x6.9in), HUD with 24 degrees angle of view, IIOTAS, storm scope WX 1000E, datalink with 10mb data streaming, helmet mounted display (HMD).

Navigation: autopilot; GPS can use a current flight plan and store another 25, all with 30 references. DME, VOR, LOC, Marker Beacon, ADF, inertial navigation. The KLN-90B independent GPS system allows the insertion of 250 waypoints.

Landing: radar altimeter, glideslope, ILS.

Communications: HF; VHF operates manually or pre-set to allow communication between aircraft and ground stations up to medium distances in a frequency range of 118,000MHz to 151,975MHz with a channel spacing of 8.33KHz and 25KHz using a Chelton V/UHF antenna and Rockwell Collins VHF-422D COMM Transceiver radio. The tactical radio is a Rohde & Schwarz XT 6313D V/UHF with encrypted data and voice transmission. The VHF has a frequency range of 225,000MHz up to 399,975MHz. For long distances an HF-ALE is used.

Attack: Laser rangefinder, CCIP, CCRP, CCIL, DTOS.

Armament, training pods, logistic and fuel tank

Armament is both conventional and precision guided. Four wing hardpoints (two on each wing) and one centreline. Inboard and centreline pylons can carry fuel tanks. Outboard wing pylons can carry 248kg (546lb) each. There is a sixth external point located under the engine where it is possible to install an EO/IR turret (FLIR Star SAFIRE I, II, III or FLIR BRITE Star II), but the EO/IR turret prevents the use of the fuselage pylon. Internally, on each wing, there is a FN Herstal M3P 12.7mm 0.5in) machine gun, with 250 rounds each. Total combat load can reach 1,550kg (3,417lb), for all variants. Central and inner stations can carry up to 351kg (773lb) of weapons or fuel tanks, while

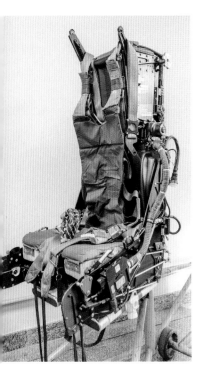

The Martin-Baker Mk BR10LCX
ejection seat.
(João Paulo Moralez)

the outer stations can carry up to 248kg (546lb). Embraer have integrated 133 weapon configurations.

Fuel tanks: The centreline fuel tank can hold 294 litres (77.66 US gal) and both combat operational underwing fuel tanks hold 317 litres (83.74 US gal) each. There are also ferry flight underwing fuel tanks capable of carrying up to 440 litres each (116 US gal), but these are for exclusive use by Embracr.

Bombs: Mk 81 119kg (262lb), BAFG-120 128kg (282lb), Mk 82 227kg (500lb), BAFG-230 248kg (546lb), M117 340kg (749lb), IAI Griffin LGB 274kg (604lb) on a Mk 82, Elbit Lizard II 250kg (551lb) on a Mk 82, GBU-58 Paveway 113kg (250lb), GBU-12 Paveway II 226kg (500lb), SUU-25F/A flare illuminator 222kg (490lb), incendiary napalm BINC-300 282kg (621lb), BLG-252 cluster bomb with 248 grenades and total mass of 324kg (714lb).

Unguided rockets: Avibras 70x7 LM70/7–SF–M9 Mk2 (LAU-32) multiple rocket launcher, up to seven 70mm (2.75in) rockets each, 47kg (103lb) empty and 125kg (275lb) loaded with Skyfire rockets, low-drag Equipaer EQ–LMF–70/7, up to seven 70mm (2.75in) rockets each, 48kg (105lb) empty and 100kg (220lb) loaded, Equipaer EQ-LMF-70/19, up to 19 70mm (2.75in) rockets each, 75kg (165lb) empty and 284kg (626lb) loaded with Skyfire rockets. Compatible with the following 70mm (2.75in) rockets: Avibras SBAT 70 7.40kg (16.31lb), Avibras Skyfire 70 M9 11kg (24.25lb), Mk 66 Hydra 70 6,2kg (13.66lb) and Advanced Precision Kill Weapons System (APKWS).

Missiles: Mectron MAA-1 Piranha air-to-air infrared guided, 89kg (196lb). Missile adapter weight 56.2kg (123lb).

Training: SUU-20 pod with up to six BEX-11 (11,3kg – 24,91lb) or six BDU-33 practice bombs and four 70mm (2.75in) rockets, with 125kg (275lb) empty and 222kg (489lb) loaded. Towed aerial target Equipaer NP-AV-1TAS 89kg (196lb), with a banner of 10m (32.8ft) length and 1,82m (5.97ft) width and 12kg (26.4lb).

Logistics: Logistic pod, 80kg (176lb) empty. 270kg (595lb) of cargo can be carried on the centre pylon.

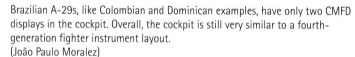

Brazilian A-29s, like Colombian and Dominican examples, have only two CMFD displays in the cockpit. Overall, the cockpit is still very similar to a fourth-generation fighter instrument layout.
(João Paulo Moralez)

One of the advantages of the EMB-314's cockpit is the generous internal space for the pilots.
(João Paulo Moralez)

▶ Afghan Air Force A-29B Super Tucano YA-1512, from the Kabul Air Wing and based at Hamid Karzai International Airport. Armed with two FN Herstal M3P 12.7mm (0.5in) machine guns with 250 rounds each, two underwing 317 litre (83.74 US gal) fuel tanks, one 119kg (262lb) Mk 81 bomb and two LAU-32 seven-tube pods for unguided 70mm (2.75in) rockets. The aircraft has external armour plates around the engine and cockpit offering protection against 12.7mm (0.5in) projectiles. Colour is Light Compass Ghost Grey (FS 36375).

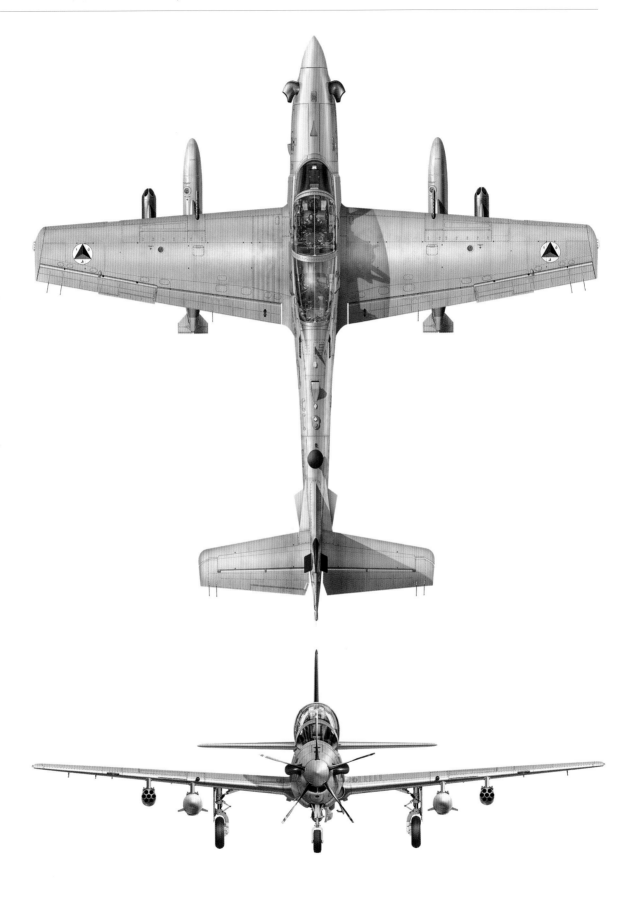

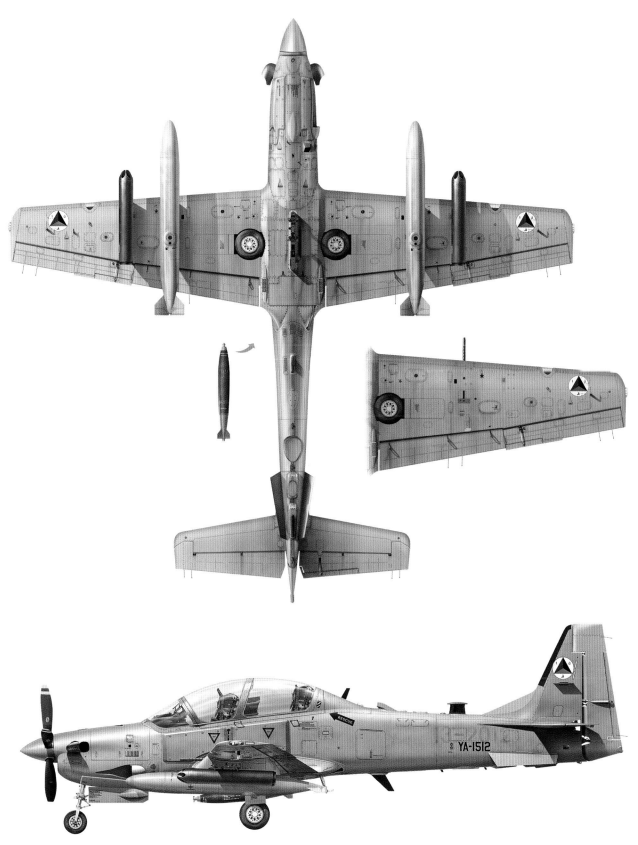

APPENDIX II: ARTWORKS

Embraer pre-studies

Four blade propeller

Garret TPE331-12B
1.100 sHP

PT-ZTW

EMB-312 c/n 312.161, registration PT-ZTW, was modified with a four-blade 1,100shp Garrett TPE331-12B engine and dive brake to serve as a demonstrator for the EMB-312G version. The idea was to offer the Brazilian Air Force a Tucano with more powerful and reinforced structure for use in training and combat missions. Colours are Red (FS 31302) and White (FS 37875).

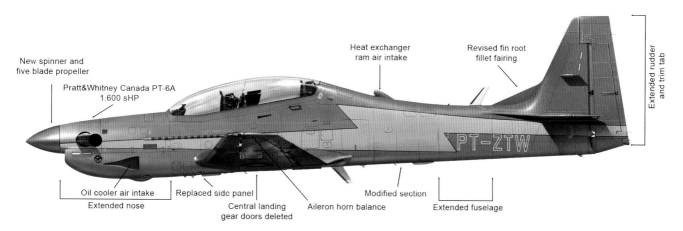

New spinner and
five blade propeller

Pratt&Whitney Canada PT-6A
1.600 sHP

Heat exchanger
ram air intake

Revised fin root
fillet fairing

Extended rudder
and trim tab

Oil cooler air intake

Extended nose

Replaced side panel

Central landing
gear doors deleted

Aileron horn balance

Modified section

Extended fuselage

PT-ZTW

To meet the JPATS contest, Embraer made major modifications to PT-ZTW including a five-blade 1,600shp Pratt & Whitney PT6A-67R and a fuselage lengthened by 1.37m (53.93in). It served as a Proof of Concept design for the upcoming JPATS programme. The aircraft received a new fin, rudder and fin root fillet fairing. OBOGS and a new air-conditioning system were also installed. Colours are Matt Pale Blue (FS 35182) and Yellow (FS 13591).

JPATS Program

PT-ZTW again, now designated EMB-312H, and with a more colourful paint scheme and two 400-litre (105-US gal) underwing fuel tanks. It was used for demonstrations in the US in July 1992, as part of the JPATS competition. Colours are Matt Pale Blue (FS 35182) and Yellow (FS 13591).

Embraer prepared two more prototypes incorporating some new features including a new clamshell canopy, a new cockpit with cathode ray tube (CRT) digital instruments, GPS, TCAS and anti-G. PT-ZTV (c/n 312.454) was used for demonstration flights in the US under the JPATS programme in September 1993. Colours are Red (FS 11136), Gloss White (FS 17925) and Dark Blue (FS 15053).

Wearing an all-gloss black paint scheme, PP-ZTV carries the NATO Flying Training in Canada logo on the fuselage after Embraer won the competition in the mid-1990s. Colour is Gloss Black (FS 27040).

Seeking to provide the Super Tucano to the Brazilian Air Force, prototype PP-ZTF (c/n 312.455) appears here wearing combat camouflage, a sharkmouth, two Mectron MAA-1 Piranha air-to-air missiles and three underwing and ventral fuel tanks of 300-litres (66-US gal) each. It made its first flight in October 1993. Colours are Gunship Grey (FS 26118) and Grey (FS 26622).

Brazilian Air Force

Brazil is the sole operator of the single-seat Super Tucano. Designated A-29A by the Brazilian Air Force, this aircraft, FAB 5702 from 1°/3° GAV 'Esquadrão Escorpião' at Boa Vista Air Force Base (now Ala 7), is equipped with a ventral 294-litre (77.66-US gal) fuel tank and two FN Herstal M3P 12.7mm (0.5in) machine gun with 250 rounds each. Note the fin with 10 years/10,000 hours logo celebrated by the squadron in 2005 as well as a blue centennial logo for Santos-Dumont's first flight. Colours are Dark Green (FS 34092) and Ocean Grey (FS 36176).

A-29B FAB 5928, from 2°/3° GAV 'Esquadrão Grifo', based at Porto Velho Air Force Base (now Ala 6), equipped with two FN Herstal M3P 12.7mm (0.5in) machine guns with 250 rounds each and one BLG-252 cluster bomb with 248 submunitions weighing 324kg (714lb). Colours are Dark Green (FS 34092) and Ocean Grey (FS 36176).

Another A-29B from 2°/3° GAV 'Esquadrão Grifo', FAB 5960, carrying two FN Herstal M3P 12.7mm (0.5in) machine guns with 250 rounds each and four BAFG-230 (248kg-546lb) bombs (similar to the Mk 82) and a ventral 294-litre (77.66-US gal.) fuel tank. Colours are Dark Green (FS 34092) and Ocean Grey (FS 36176).

EQUIPAER EQ-LMF-70 WITHOUT ROCKETS

3°/3° GAV 'Esquadrão Flecha' A-29A FAB 5713 is heavily armed for an attack mission, with two FN Herstal M3P 12.7mm (0.5in) machine guns with 250 rounds each, one ventral 294-litre (77.66-US gal) fuel tank and four Equipaer EQ-LMF-70/19 pods for 19 70mm (2.75in) unguided rockets. Colours are Dark Green (FS 34092) and Ocean Grey (FS 36176).

3°/3° GAV 'Esquadrão Flecha', based at Campo Grande Air Force Base (now Ala 5) is equipped with both single- and two-seat Super Tucanos. Here, A-29B FAB 5931 is equipped with two FN Herstal M3P 12.7mm (0.5in) machine guns with 250 rounds each, two underwing 317-litre (83.74-US gal) fuel tanks and a FLIR Star SAFIRE II EO/IR turret. Colours are Dark Green (FS 34092) and Ocean Grey (FS 36176).

At 2°/5° GAV, Super Tucanos can also carry an Equipaer NP-AV-1TAS ventral air target pod for a towed banner that supports 20mm, 30mm and 50mm calibre impacts. Here, FAB 5916 also has two underwing 317-litre (83.74-US gal) fuel tanks and two FN Herstal M3P 12.7mm (0.5in) machine guns with 250 rounds each. Colours are Dark Green (FS 34092) and Ocean Grey (FS 36176).

From 2013 to 2015, A-29A 'Blue 1' FAB 5734 belonged to Lieutenant-Colonel Marcelo Gobett Cardoso, the first commander of the Esquadrilha da Fumaça once the team converted to the Super Tucano. The specialist official was Major Specialist Márcio Aparecido Tonisso. Stationed at Pirassununga, São Paulo. Colour is overall Blue (FS 15095).

The In-Flight Research and Testing Institute, based at São José dos Campos, has two A-29Bs for research purposes and test pilot training. Here, FAB 5924 has a test probe and no machine guns. These can be added if the mission requires. Note the telemetry antennas just in front of the cockpit, above and below the fuselage. Colours are Dark Green (FS 34092) and Ocean Grey (FS 36176).

Foreign operators

Afghan Air Force A-29B YA-1408 has a weapons load typical for a local COIN mission. Based at Hamid Karzai International Airport, it is armed with two FN Herstal M3P 12.7mm (0.5in) machine guns with 250 rounds each, three 119kg (262lb) Mk 81 bombs and two 317-litre (83.74-US gal) fuel tanks. The aircraft has external armour plates at the engine and cockpit for protection against 12.7mm projectiles. Colour is Light Compass Ghost Grey (FS 36375).

The National Air Force of Angola bases its Super Tucano fleet at Catumbela Air Base, where they serve Regimento Aéreo de Caças-Bombardeiros (Fighter Bomber Air Regiment). R-704, a two-seater, is equipped with two FN Herstal M3P 12.7mm (0.5in) machine guns with 250 rounds each and one 294-litre (77.66-US gal) centreline fuel tank. Colours are Medium Grey (FS 26300), Tan (FS 20219), Dark Green (FS 24095), Black (FS 27038).

Stationed at Base Aérienne 210 at Bobo-Dioulasso with Escadrille de Chasse (Fighter Squadron), this Burkina Air Force two-seat Super Tucano is equipped with two FN Herstal M3P 12.7mm (0.5in) machine guns with 250 rounds each and two LAU-32 seven-tube pods for 70mm (2.75in) unguided rockets. BF 1103 wears Green (FS 24227), Light Green (FS 26480) and Admiral Blue (FS 25440).

Chilean Air Force two-seat Super Tucanos belong to Grupo de Aviación No. 1 (Aviation Grupo No. 1) at Los Condores Air Base, Iquique. FACh 456 is displayed with two FN Herstal M3P 12.7mm (0.5in) machine guns with 250 rounds each, two 317-litre (83.74-US gal) fuel tanks under the wings and one ventral 294-litre (77.66-US gal) tank. Colours are Green (FS 24097), Tan (FS 20219), Dark Green (FS 24064) and rudder in Blue (FS 25048).

First export customer for the Super Tucano was the Colombian Air Force. Two-seat EMB-314 FAC 3103 is from Escuadrón de Combate 211 'Grifos' (Combat Squadron 211 'Grifos') based at Apiay, Meta. Armed with two 340kg (750lb) M117 bombs, two FN Herstal M3P 12.7mm (0.5in) machine guns with 250 rounds each and one ventral fuel tank of 294 litres (77.66 US gal), this aircraft is wearing a two-tone camouflage of Ocean Grey (FS 26173) and Grey (FS 26293).

Escuadrón de Combate 312 'Drakos' (Combat Squadron 312 'Drakos'), at Malambo, Barranquilla, was the second unit to receive the Super Tucano. FAC 3123 is armed with four Mk 82 227kg (500lb) bombs, one ventral fuel tank of 294 litres (77.66 US gal) and two FN Herstal M3P 12.7mm (0.5in) machine guns with 250 rounds each. It wears a two-tone camouflage of Ocean Grey (FS 26173) and Grey (FS 26293).

Dominican Republic Super Tucanos are quite similar to those of the Brazilian Air Force in terms of equipment and avionics. Here, two-seat FAD 2904 from Escuadrón de Combate 'Dragones' (Combat Squadron 'Dragons') at San Isidro Air Force Base carries two FN Herstal M3P 12.7mm (0.5in) machine guns with 250 rounds each and a ventral 294-litre (77.66-US gal) fuel tank. Colours are Ocean Grey (FS 26173) and Grey (FS 26293).

Based at Manta Air Force Base, with Escuadrón de Combate 2313 'Halcones' (Combat Squadron 2313 'Hawks'), all Ecuadorian Super Tucanos are two-seaters and among the most advanced versions in the world. FAE 1018 'El Oro' is armed with two FN Herstal M3P 12.7mm (0.5in) machine guns with 250 rounds each, one ventral fuel tank of 294-litres (77.66-US gal) and four Elbit Lizard II laser-guided bombs. Colours are Light Grey (FS 26495), Medium Grey (FS 26300), Tan (FS 20219), Dark Green (FS 24095), Black (FS 27038), Dark Green (FS 24036) and Brown (FS 24080).

The Indonesian Air Force fleet is based at Abdul Rachman Saleh Air Base, Malang, with Skadron Udara 21 (Air Squadron 21). TT-3102 is armed with two FN Herstal M3P 12.7mm (0.5in) machine guns with 250 rounds each, four Mk 81 119kg (250lb) bombs and one 294-litre (77.66-US gal) centreline fuel tank. Colours are Dark Sea Grey (FS 26152) and Grey (FS 26293).

Stationed at Hamat Air Force Base, in Batroun, with 7th Squadron, Lebanese Air Force Super Tucanos are the most advanced version currently in operation. With external armour plates for protection against 12.7mm (0.5in) projectiles around the engine and cockpit, L-711 is equipped with two FN Herstal M3P 12.7mm (0.5in) machine guns with 250 rounds each and two 113kg (250lb) Elbit Lizard II laser-guided bombs. Colour is Light Compass Ghost Grey (FS 36375) with low-visibility markings.

Escadrille de Chasse (Fighter Squadron) based at Base Aérienne 102 at Mopti, Malian Air Force, will receive two-seat Super Tucanos with external armour plates around the engine and cockpit. TZ-01C is equipped with two FN Herstal M3P 12.7mm (0.5in) machine guns with 250 rounds each and is wearing a scheme of Dark Sand (FS 22563), Light Sand (FS 23613) and Admiral Blue (FS 25440).

Flown by the Mauritanian Super Tucano Squadron, this is part of the very active fleet of A-29Bs at Base Aérienne 210, Atar. 5T-MAW 192 is equipped with two underwing 317-litre (83.74-US gal) fuel tanks, one 294-litre (77.66-US gal) ventral fuel tank, two FN Herstal M3P 12.7mm (0.5in) machine guns with 250 rounds each and two LAU-32 seven-tube pods for 70mm (2.75in) unguided rockets. It wears wrap-around Light Ivory (RAL 1015) and Beige (RAL 1001).

EP Aviation LLC, a subsidiary of the controversial security company Blackwater, leased two-seat Super Tucano c/n 31400082 to participate in the USN Imminent Fury programme. It was heavily modified with new avionics and tested over a year. Here, it has the inscription 'Fury', the VAL-4 'Black Ponies' attack squadron badge, civilian registration N314TG and fake military registration 163056. It is equipped with two FN Herstal M3P 12.7mm (0.5in) machine guns with 250 rounds each, BRITE STAR II EO/IR turret and two seven-tube pods for 70mm (2.75in) unguided rockets. It wears overall Medium Grey (FS 16628).

After evaluation by the USN, N314TG stayed with Xe Aviation LLC, the new name of the Blackwater subsidiary. On 30 November 2012 it was sold to Tactical Air Support Inc. for private military training programmes. Here is equipped with two underwing 317-litre (83.74-US gal) tanks, no machine guns and is wearing overall Medium Grey (FS 16628).

Before delivery to the Afghan Air Force, the fleet of A-29Bs was operated by the USAF's 81st Fighter Squadron at Moody Air Force Base, where flight training was provided to Afghan pilots. A-29B 13-2001 is seen here with its Afghan serial number still covered, and the name Lt Colonel Jeffrey 'Growler' Hogan, then 81st FS commander, written under the windshield. It is armed with two FN Herstal M3P 12.7mm (0.5in) machine guns with 250 rounds each and two underwing 317-litre (83.74-US gal) fuel tanks. The aircraft has external armour plates around the engine and cockpit. Colour is Light Compass Ghost Grey (FS 36375).

EMB-312 Tucano | Brazil's turboprop success story

João Paulo Zeitoun Moralez

256 pages, 28×21 cm, softcover

35.95 Euro, ISBN 978-0-9973092-3-2

The story of Embraer's EMB-312 turboprop trainer, the first aircraft in its class and a market leader that was sold to 16 countries and produced under licence in the United Kingdom. Comprehensive details are provided of local and foreign service, combat operations, as well as a full inventory of EMB-312 units and insignia.

Modern Chinese Warplanes | Chinese Naval Aviation – Aircraft and Units

Andreas Rupprecht

96 pages, 28×21 cm, softcover

18.95 Euro, ISBN 978-09973092-5-6

China's 2016 white paper emphasised a greater focus on the seas and clearly states the country's ambition to establish itself as a major maritime power. Consequently, the People's Liberation Naval Air Force will shift its focus from defence of offshore waters to 'open seas protection'. The changes for Naval Aviation, the focus of this book, will probably be even more dramatic than those for the air force. It will increase its capabilities by introducing more modern, multirole-capable systems and, most importantly, establish a carrier force. As well as the most important aircraft and weapons in Naval Aviation service, this compact and lavishly illustrated directory includes aircraft markings and serial number systems, recent modernisation efforts, structural reforms and orders of battle.

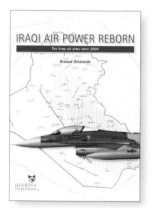

Iraqi Air Power Reborn | The Iraqi air arms since 2004

Arnaud Delalande

80 pages, 28×21 cm, softcover

18.95 Euro, ISBN 978-0-9854554-7-7

Iraqi Air Power Reborn provides the most authoritative account of the Iraqi air arms in the years following Operation Iraqi Freedom. In the space of over a decade since Harpia Publishing presented its groundbreaking and ever-popular *Iraqi Fighters*, the Iraqi Air Force has undergone an unprecedented transformation. Having been almost entirely decimated by coalition air strikes in 2003, and during the insurgency that followed, Baghdad has set about rebuilding its air power from scratch. This book summarises the history of the Iraqi Air Force and its various incarnations until 2003 before detailing the efforts to establish a new-look Air Force, which began with training formations, before adding transport and reconnaissance squadrons, and finally attack and fighter squadrons. Coverage also extends to Iraqi Army Aviation, and its various transport, special operations, armed reconnaissance and attack squadrons, as well as the latest air operations against the so-called Islamic State.